Also by this Author

Outrageous Prayer

What Other Christian Leaders Are Saying...

This is such a powerful book, full of insight and developmental teaching. I'm excited that it's in your hand! *The Search For More* explores the longing desire of the human heart, its need for purpose, meaning, and its driving pursuit in the quest for true contentment, and abiding joy. Each chapter will invite you to sweetly linger over concepts, contrasts, and our need for truth. In the pause of contemplative discovery, David builds our understanding on why so many of our lifelong pursuits, although good and purposeful, often feel fruitless, empty, and leave us dissatisfied. Laying a strong foundation, our need for Jesus, and the necessity of His teachings, David pulls on scripture and narrative to re-set the reader's life towards meaningful pursuit and a life of fruitful satisfaction. Be delightfully prepared to come "undone" only to re-boot and live again!

Theresa Farrelly, Business owner, Dallas, Oregon, Pastor, New Horizons Church McMinnville, Oregon

David Freitag has captured in his new book what I hear God saying to the greater Church. God is calling Christians to a deeper love and intimacy with Him. In doing so, God desires His children to change the way they think, to move on from cultural empty promises, and develop a Kingdom mindset. The Christian life is an abundant life in the Kingdom which calls Christians to become an ambassador to the unsaved and to the earth. Freitag's book aims to empower the reader to change their mindset and their lives to fulfill God-given callings. This is a very powerful book and I need to read it again. I highly recommend the book.

>Dr. Joel Collier, Associate Pastor, Abiding Place Christian Fellowship, Portland, Oregon

For those who are hungry for the sincere meat of the Bible, David is uniquely gifted in breaking open the Word of God to new depths and fresh insight. In this book he takes a given subject, and with a skillful weaving of scripture together, creates a beautiful picture as he blends scripture together, you will know beyond doubt, you are on very, very good solid scriptural ground that will stand the test of the battles around you.

We highly recommend *The Search for More*, and know it will be a great blessing to all who read it.

Stan and Ellen Mishler, Pastors, New Horizons Church, McMinnville, Oregon

Search for More is a compelling, persuasive, and practical commentary that invites believers to live life fully alive in Christ. David Freitag does a wonderful job of leading the reader to discover the contentment of being known by the Father. This book stirs a hunger for God to speak into our desires and to encounter the more that He has promised. David is a deep thinker and his strong teaching gift emerges as you engage with the content on these pages. I am honored to be able to recommend this book that releases keys to bearing fruit in our journey with God.

Micah Burns, Pastor, Beach Chapel, Encinitas, California

THE SEARCH FOR MORE

Finding True Contentment When Good Things Fail Us

DAVID FREITAG

The Search For More by David Freitag

Copyright © 2021 David Freitag.

All rights reserved in all countries No part of this book may be reproduced in any form or by any electronic or mechanical means including information storage and retrieval systems without the prior written permission of the author, except by a reviewer who may quote brief passages in a review, or as otherwise permitted by current copyright law.

ISBN: 978-1-7373126-0-4

Cover design Hackntog LLC

Printed in the United States of America.

*This book is dedicated to my instructors,
who all helped me understand Scripture
and grasp how it was applicable to my life.*

Foreword

I highly recommend this book for all people who seek accelerated growth beyond traditional religious thinking and practices which rob the soul of the pleasure of knowing God. *The Search for More* clearly illustrates the distinct differences between the values of this world versus the values of God's kingdom. David Freitag superbly lays out a pathway of living that leads to abiding joy and rewards in this life, which all of humanity longs to experience. Personal stories, woven masterfully throughout dozens of biblical references and teachings, create a spiritual hunger to discover how to live a powerful and successful life, God's way.

Galen Gingerich, Sr. Leader
    New Horizons Church
    McMinnville, Oregon

Introduction

Three thousand years ago, a wealthy man—who was also likely the wisest man who ever lived—wrote down some thoughts about life. Being both wealthy and wise, he had the opportunity to explore what people believed would make them happy. He came to the conclusion that all pursuits were found wanting in the area of satisfying the human heart. Although each individual pursuit was not necessarily evil—and many of them were good—these pursuits were still limited in that they could not bring fulfillment. The wealthy and wise man, Solomon, concluded that everything is ultimately meaningless. He concluded that humankind's lifelong pursuit to find meaning and purpose often comes up empty. The question is, "why?" Why do even good pursuits lack lasting satisfaction to humanity?

The answer seems to lie in the fact that people continually search for meaning in places they believe will provide satisfaction. But such efforts wind up disillusioning them. The driving force behind the world's deception of humankind is connected to individuals believing the lie that they can do something, acquire something, or become someone that will give them lasting fulfillment. People seek lasting satisfaction through various means, some of which are good, but the unsatiated desire for meaning is what causes such pursuits to feel fruitless. Those who seek purpose in the wrong ways may do great things, even becoming wealthy and famous, but in the end, the seeker typically remains empty. Believing that human pursuits can bring satisfaction is a continuing lie from the Garden of Eden. Eve was told that, through disobedience, she would be like God and find purpose. But only those who seek to honor Jesus find the joy of peace and contentment.

The enemy lies to us, saying we must leave an imprint for people to remember us. Yet, it's not ourselves that we should seek to promote. If we insist on self-promotion, we will continually be driven to disappointment. Rather, it's God's name that we are to promote. As we lift up Jesus' name, then we will also be drawing ourselves up with him.

As we examine the life of Jesus, we discover a completely different way of being. The apostle John wrote that if we love the world, the love of God cannot be in us, because the world's type of love is in direct opposition to God's type of love (1 John 2:15-17). Yet, what does it mean to "love the world"? It doesn't mean that we don't care for the world, because John 3:16 tells us that God loved the world so much that he gave Jesus, his son, to die so that those who believed in him would not perish. However, to the extent that our lifestyles differ from that of Jesus, that's how much more we love the world. Jesus perfectly loved the Father (who I will refer to as simply "Father," or "our Father" from this point forward, to evoke greater intimacy) so that he could say to his disciple, Philip, that anyone who has seen him (Jesus) has also seen Father. In other words, Jesus perfectly lived out love for God and the love of God. That means any deviation from the way Jesus lived is a deviation from how we are to live. Jesus told the Jews that he only did what he saw Father doing. Such a statement means Jesus' will was completely and perfectly in submission to that of Father (John 5:39) and that he perfectly lived out the Lord's Prayer, "your will be done on earth as it is in heaven."

The reason we often do not live with the power Jesus displayed is our lack of grasping Father's will, revealed to each one of us by Holy Spirit who dwells in every follower of Jesus. Often, the reason we fail to discern and submit to Holy Spirit's revelation of Father's heart is because we still have a desire to follow the world, live like it, and receive recognition as well as praise from others. So, we, as Solomon explored three thousand years ago, discover that living as the world lives is meaningless. Yet, we still wonder why we don't see the same powerful works that Jesus performed and said that his followers would do (John 14:12).

Why do we continually choose to love and follow the world? I believe it is largely due to a lack of closeness with the Father. Jesus and Father shared an intimate relationship, so Jesus understood that doing Father's will on earth was more satisfying than anything we could do to make a name for ourselves. As we grow in intimacy with Father, at least two things happen. First, our trust in him grows. It cannot help but grow, because as our revelation of the living God increases and his perfect love for us is more completely revealed, we can do nothing but trust him more. We become like the child who, over time, continually experiences the benefits of knowing his father. As time goes on, the child's trust in him grows. Second, we discover more and more what Father wants done in our lives. As we live out what he wants and submit what we want, just like Jesus did, we see more of the same things in our lives that Jesus did. Jesus healed the sick, cast out demons, raised the dead, and calmed the storms because he was in perfect and intimate communion with Father. He did exactly what Father wanted done in any given situation, so that all those for whom Jesus prayed received exactly what they needed—because it was Father's heart. As we approach intimacy with our Father, we will also see the Spirit do the same things through us that he did through Jesus.

The purpose of this book is to consider the ways many good things fail to provide what the human heart desires—and in it, we will take a look at some of what the Bible teaches about true contentment as well as seeing it developed in our lives.

Contents

1. Making a Name for Yourself Comes Up Short — 1
2. Education Does Not Always Give Us What We Think It Gives — 15
3. Entertainment Leaves Us Empty — 28
4. Money and Possessions Are Given to Bless Others — 38
5. The Pursuit of Jesus is Worth Everything — 51
6. How to Sustain Lasting Joy — 71
7. The Veil Has Been Removed — 87
8. Being Transformed Through Relationship — 101
9. Living Out a Transformed Life — 109
10. Living Out Kingdom Greatness — 120
11. Applying Kingdom Greatness — 131
12. Striving in the Right Way — 140
13. Father's Unfathomable Love for Us — 151
14. Jesus Defeats Despair — 163
15. Prophetic Crossroads Determine Our Future — 176
16. How Are We to Understand the Fear of the Lord? — 185
17. Conclusions — 194

Acknowledgments — 205
About the Author — 207

ONE

Making a Name for Yourself Comes Up Short

NOT MANY OF us would recognize the name, Jerusha Edwards. In life, she was not famous. She never made a name for herself, and she didn't have a career as we would define it. She never married, never had children, and never did any of those things the world says are so important. She didn't even live to see her eighteenth birthday. Nevertheless, she had impact because she brought honor to Jesus. In the spring of 1747, a young missionary showed up at her family's home. He was quite ill, and seventeen-year-old Jerusha took up the task of caring for him. For nineteen weeks, she cared for this young man. In October of 1747, he died of tuberculosis, which he had previously contracted while proclaiming Jesus' love to the Native Americans of New England. Several months later, Jerusha died from the same disease, which she had contracted from the missionary. However, due to her care, the young missionary was able to complete his diary and leave it with Jerusha's father for publication. That diary has never been out of print in over 250 years. The young missionary was David Brainerd, whose diary has inspired many Christians over the last two centuries; but without Jerusha, he likely would not have finished it.

While we on earth may not remember Jerusha Edwards or those who have similarly given their lives to serve others, our Papa in heaven never forgets what they have done. Jerusha's life and death remind us of what is truly important in life; she demonstrated the value of service and relationship. Her life is in direct contrast to what our world declares to be important: education, wealth, fame, and accomplishment. Yet, we are continually tempted and encouraged to make names for ourselves, to promote all that we have done and can do.

Ironically, how we live today is eerily similar to a biblical society described in Genesis 11:4. What drove the people of Babel to build their tower was that they might make a name for themselves, and it was that desire that led God to confuse their language. I doubt that many of us would consider the desire to make names for ourselves something that our Papa in heaven would find disturbing. Many assume that doing so is what we are supposed to do in life. For many, it is absurd to even suggest that we are not to make great names for ourselves. However, the story of Babel reveals that their desire to make a name for themselves was disturbing to him. That being the case, we should explore why such a desire in our hearts might be disturbing to our Father.

We know from Scripture that Father loves us and desires the very best for his children. This is the place to begin. To comprehend why the desire to make names for ourselves is disturbing to Father, we must grasp who we are. The Gospel of John reveals to us that if we are in

Christ, then we have received the right to be called children of God (John 1:12). As children of God, we know from Jesus' teaching in the Lord's Prayer that it is our privilege to call God our Father, our Papa, our Daddy. As his children, then, we have the right to be called by his name. As such, we have a great privilege and honor to uphold.

Some time ago, I heard a story about the British Royal Princes William and Harry. They were with their mother, Princess Diana. At a certain point, William, impressed by the role of a policeman, declared to his mother and brother that he desired to become a policeman. As such, he would give protection to his mother and family. His younger brother, Harry, quickly informed him that it was impossible for him to be a policeman since he was a prince. I am not sure this story is true or accurate, but it illustrates a very important point—how odd it would be for a prince to trade his identity as a prince to become a policeman. That doesn't mean that being a policeman is not important, but being a policeman is not the same as being a prince. It would not be appropriate for someone with greater responsibility to deny who he is and take a position of lesser responsibility.

When you and I give in to the temptation to make names for ourselves, we have then denied the great privilege of who we are in relationship to our Father. Paul declared to the Philippians that Jesus had been given the name that is above every other name—that at his name every knee would bow and every tongue confess him as Lord (Philippians 2:9-11). Jesus prayed that we would share the same glory that he himself had, the same glory that he had with Father before he became a man (John

17:20-24). Do we really think we could make names for ourselves that are greater than the name of God? Do we really think that we can make our own names more glorious than what we already have through Jesus? If not, then why would any of us desire to make names for ourselves?

At times, a believer may not understand what they find in their own heart. The believer recognizes that there are times when they desire to be recognized and honored. In our world, people are recognized by position as well as possessions and money, and the more money that one makes in a given period of time reflects how valuable he or she is to the world. According to the world, the nicer possessions that someone has says something about his or her value. Positions held also say something about the individual's value. According to the world, the executive receives more honor than the custodian. The executive commands a higher salary, lives in a finer house, and is asked for their opinion more frequently than the custodian. This is the way of the world, and there is inherently a part of many of us that would rather live like the executive than the custodian. The question is, why? If we already have relationship with Jesus, bear God's name, and are princes and princesses, why would we yearn for more than that? A desire for the world's recognition reveals a higher value for the world's opinion than heaven's.

Why do we desire this? Jesus said things like it is easier for a camel to pass through the eye of a needle than it is for a rich man to enter into the kingdom of heaven (Luke 18:23-25). Unless we become like little children, we can never enter into the kingdom of heaven (Matthew 18:1-3). James wrote to the rich, telling them to weep and to wail for the way they had neglected the poor (James 5:1-4). Nevertheless, most of us would rather be rich than poor, would rather have more than less, would rather have a position of honor than be overlooked.

Many would agree that Jesus' relatively short life had greater impact than any person who has ever lived. Yet, in his day, he neither had nor did any of the things that declared a person's life to have had value. Jesus came from a country and a region that was poor and often held in contempt. If he lived today, Jesus probably wouldn't be an American, because America is the Rome of the modern world. He would likely be a person who came from the developing world. How many of us would follow a person who wasn't "successful" according to the world's standards? Although Jesus didn't have an impressive citizenship on earth, he has given to you and me citizenship in heaven (Philippians 3:20). During his entire ministry, he lived the life of a homeless person. When a man came to follow Jesus, affirming that he would follow Jesus anywhere, Jesus reminded him that "foxes have dens and birds have nests, but the Son of Man has no place to lay his head" (Matthew 8:20). How many of us would listen to a person who lived as a homeless man today? Nevertheless, Jesus promises us that he goes to prepare a place for us in our Father's home (John 14:1-3). The entire time Jesus ministered, he received no salary, nor income, for what he did. In effect, he was unemployed. Although Jesus had no earthly income, he tells us that those of us who follow him will inherit the kingdom of heaven and the earth (Matthew 5:3-5). Even Jesus' brothers rebuked him for his lack of promoting himself and suggested he show himself to the world in order to become known (John 7:1-8).

Jesus perfectly fulfilled what Isaiah had said about him. Over 800 years before Jesus was born, Isaiah had written that the Messiah would have no form nor appearance that would attract us to him (Isaiah 53:2). In other words, today, Jesus would be a homeless, unemployed man from a developing nation who taught spiritual truth. We have to wonder if we would have even noticed him. Outside of Palestine, he went unnoticed in his own day.

Or consider the apostle Paul. Paul had everything Jesus didn't have. He had a position as a Pharisee. He had honor and respect from all those the world says we should gain respect from. He had Roman citizenship. He had an education. He likely came from a wealthy family who could send him from Tarsus to Jerusalem for an education. But what did Paul say about all these privileges? He said that he counted them all as rubbish. He compared them to what should be thrown out, because they are dirty and stink things up. (Philippians 3:7-10). It's no wonder Paul gained no sympathy from his former friends and colleagues, because he disregarded everything they believed to be important and of value. Adding to their disdain, he chose to follow a man they declared to be an annoying nobody from Nazareth. Furthermore, Paul kept doing signs and wonders, similar to those of Jesus, which confirmed his message. It shouldn't surprise us that Paul's former friends and colleagues wanted him dead.

When we lived in Italy, we observed some uniquely Italian modes of transportation, all the way from Ferraris, which cost over a hundred thousand dollars, to Vespas, which cost several thousand. It would be absurd for a

Ferrari—while stuck in Neapolitan traffic—to seek to be transformed into a Vespa just because a Vespa can go up on the sidewalk and weave in and out of traffic. However, we often do the same thing. As followers of Jesus, we've been given a name and a position that is of priceless value. Nevertheless, we often desire to make names for ourselves, because that is what we see others doing, and it seems most convenient at the time.

On the other hand, consider how successful those who seek to make a name for themselves really are. The key to making a name for yourself is that you will be remembered — that people will know who you are. So, let's consider some significant achievements in the world's eyes.

In the sporting world, winning a championship is the pinnacle. Can you remember who was the winning pitcher of the final game of last year's World Series? Can you name the team that won the World Series two years ago? Now, what about football? Who was the MVP of the Super Bowl two years ago? In the world of horse racing, what is the name of the jockey who rode the winning horse of the Kentucky Derby three years ago?

Maybe you're not a sports fan, that's OK. So, what about entertainment? In the world of entertainment: Who won the Oscar for best actor two years ago? Who had the most popular song six months ago? Who directed the movie that won the best picture last year? All of these people have made names for themselves. However, their accomplishments are forgotten in a relatively short period of time.

Maybe sports and entertainment are not important to you, but history of your country certainly must be. For example, who were Chester Arthur and John Tyler? Although these men may not be household names, in their day and in our nation, they made names for themselves. Each was a President of the United States. Chester Arthur was the twenty-first and John Tyler the tenth.

Each of these individuals "made a name for themselves," and most of us have no idea who they are. In some cases, just a few months after they were at the pinnacle of their profession, they are largely forgotten by the public. Can we agree that making a name for yourself is not exactly what it's cracked up to be?

This desire to make names for ourselves leads us to address why we are uncomfortable with fully trusting our heavenly Father and *his* purpose for us. Sometime ago, I discovered a quote from General Douglas MacArthur about the value of being a father. It struck me that I had never heard of his son—that I didn't even know his name. So, I did some research. Apparently, General MacArthur had wanted his son, Arthur, to attend West Point and become a general like himself and his own father, the Civil War General Arthur MacArthur. However, young Arthur didn't want to follow that path. He attended Columbia University. After his father died, he changed his name and has apparently lived his life as a musician in relative obscurity.

In studying the relationship between Douglas and Arthur MacArthur, I found some interesting parallels and contrasts to our relationship with our Father in heaven. Like Arthur MacArthur, we have a very famous Father who loves us deeply and has plans and purposes for our lives. However, where Douglas MacArthur perhaps did not fully understand his son, this is not our case. Our

Father understands us perfectly, even better than we understand ourselves. Nevertheless, his plans for us may not coincide with what we think we need. We have the strange tendency to view what others have and are and want that for ourselves, not fully appreciating what our Father has given to us and built into us.

At times, we may fear that God will make us do something we don't want to do. So, we desire to become something or someone we are not. In so doing, we forget important truths. God our Father is not against us. Therefore, we do not need to assume his plans will make us miserable. Furthermore, perhaps that thing we believe will make us miserable may actually be what our Father created us to be.

Many of us are in situations we never thought we would be in. I never wanted to, nor thought I would ever regularly find myself speaking in front of groups of people, much less work for many years as a pastor. In high school, I was petrified of giving speeches to my class. I got tongue tied and couldn't think straight. Even today, I get nervous if asked to introduce myself in a small group setting. Yet, God has given me opportunities to share what he has taught me, and I've grown to enjoy doing so. I've learned and continue to learn that there is great value in trusting the love and plans that my Father has for me; then I am free from the burden of having to make a name for myself, because the name and identity I have received is far superior to what I could achieve for myself.

The lives of Jerusha Edwards, Jesus, and Paul teach us an important spiritual truth that is hinted at in Hebrews 12:1-2. The author of Hebrews describes life on earth as a great stadium with a heavenly audience cheering us on.

He uses imagery from the Roman games to display athletic prowess. Today, we would say that earth is a great stadium, and you and I are on the playing field—it is the Super Bowl, the World Series, or the Olympics. To use another metaphor, earth is Carnegie Hall, and as you live out your life to honor Papa and Jesus, you are playing a grand symphony for all of heaven to enjoy. Earth is the Louvre in Paris, the Uffizi in Florence, or the Vatican Museums in Rome where people come from all over the world to observe the masterpieces of great artists. However, in our case, the audience is not people on earth; it is all of heaven. Life is not about obtaining the praise of other individuals. If it were, Jerusha, Jesus, and Paul wasted their lives, because the men and the women of their day didn't honor them.

The key question, then, is not what the people of Babel asked and what modern individuals ask. How do I make a name for myself? How do I get noticed? Rather, the important question is: What is it that causes heaven to applaud my life? What is it that Papa desires for me? Let's look at some things Jesus said are important.

Jesus' teaching on prayer in the Sermon on the Mount is actually part of a greater truth found in Matthew 6. We are not to live our lives for the purpose of being praised by people, but to seek the praise of our Father alone. In other words, we are to develop our relationship with Father when we are alone with him. To illustrate that principle, Jesus taught his disciples the importance of helping the poor in secret. Actually, it is not done in secret, because Father sees, which also means all of heaven sees what has been done. That whole crowd of witnesses, of which the author of Hebrews wrote, is observing. It is just that we may not notice their attention. When we help someone in need and no other person is aware of what we have done, we reveal that we have truly done it to honor Father and not for humans to praise us and honor us. Every day and every part of every day, we are to choose the right thing to do for the sake of others, as if that person were Jesus himself.

Jesus went on to explain that we are not to seek attention when we pray in public—but rather, we are to take advantage of those times when, in secret, we delight in the presence of Father and express to him the dreams and aspirations of our heart. It is interesting to consider the possibility that when we have the world's attention, we are backstage in heaven, and when we are offstage in the world, we are in heaven's spotlight.

Later in the Gospel of Matthew, Jesus declared the importance of helping the weak (Matthew 10:42; 18:5). When we help those who could never return the favor to us, we reveal the kingdom on earth, because this is Father's heart toward us. This is the gospel. Jesus gave to us eternal life. We can never return anything of equal value back to him. He did for us what we could not do for ourselves.

I think of a young woman raised in affluence in Southern California. She got married and, with her husband, she went to the mission field. After some years, she and her husband had the opportunity to get their PhD's from Oxford in England. Now, when you get a PhD from Oxford, you don't have to look for a job, because employers come looking for you. But instead of teaching in a university, they chose to go to Africa and work with orphans. Through them, signs and wonders broke out, the deaf began to hear, and the blind regained their sight. In a predominantly Muslim nation, many turned their lives to Jesus. The vast majority of the world has never heard of Heidi and Rolland Baker, but their lives are examples of what it means to follow Jesus.

I wonder how often David Brainerd, as he lay in bed during the final weeks of his life, was tempted to think his life was a waste. He was prevented from completing his education at Yale. He never became an ordained minister. He had only four years of ministry, and even that was of questionable value in the eyes of others. Nevertheless, it is David Brainerd who is now remembered more than the famous instructors of Yale who made the decision to expel him. Brainerd is remembered for his diary and the experiences he wrote in it more than the sermons he preached to the Native Americans. In other words, it might be that thing we do in secret, that sacrifice we make when we don't think anyone notices, which becomes the real reason for our life.

Consider Mary, the sister of Lazarus. In John 12, we read of her approaching Jesus six days before his death. She brought a pound of pure nard, an expensive perfume, and she poured the entire amount upon Jesus, filling the room with the fragrance of the perfume. Unfortunately, Judas began to criticize her for what appeared to him an expensive waste of money that could have been spent on the poor. However, as John pointed out, Judas made those remarks, not out of concern for the poor, but because he wanted some of the money for himself. Nevertheless, the other eleven disciples joined him in their criticism of Mary until Jesus told them all to knock it off. What Mary had done was a preparation for his burial. She should be praised, not criticized. However, if you read Mark's account of the same event, Jesus added that Mary would be forever remembered for what she had done. Wherever the gospel is preached, what Mary had done would be told as a memorial of her love and affection for Jesus (Mark 14:6-9).

Mary's example teaches us that if Jesus wants you remembered, you cannot be forgotten! Most of us struggle to remember the names of all twelve of the disciples. We remember Peter, James, and John. We remember Judas because he betrayed Jesus. Most of the time, we remember Thomas, because he doubted. However, after that, we arrive at the "oh yeah disciples": "Oh yeah, Philip" and "Oh, yeah, Andrew." The guys who criticized Mary and had the position of being disciples are often forgotten; but we remember Mary, because Jesus declared she would never be forgotten.

The more I reflect, the more it occurs to me that, often, we do not have the foggiest idea of what Father is doing and accomplishing in our lives. People of significance in the world's eyes are often forgotten, while the Marys, the David Brainerds, and the Jerusha Edwards are remembered in the kingdom.

All of us want to leave a lasting impact. The way to do so is to not be worried about promoting ourselves or seeking what the world seeks, but to give ourselves completely to promoting the kingdom and to promoting Jesus. Then, whatever happens will be because Jesus is doing it. If Jesus is doing it, then it will last and be remembered.

Questions for Reflection

1. In what ways does the world's pursuit of recognition impact and distract you from the kingdom of God?
2. How are you developing your relationship with Father? In what ways might you deepen your relationship with him?
3. Why do you think so many have a strong desire to be recognized by others?

TWO

Education Does Not Always Give Us
What We Think It Gives

FOR MANY YEARS, I believed the acquisition of knowledge would lead to happiness and contentment. Neither my parents nor any relatives of their generation graduated from college. Consequently, my dad always encouraged my sister and me to get a university degree. We both have passed that value down to our children. Having gone to college and graduate school, with a former dream of going back for a doctorate, I am one who has valued education—and I still do. However, for many years, I lived according to the belief that the more I studied, particularly the Bible, the closer I would be to God. I associated the accumulation of knowledge and the acquisition of an education with happiness. I spent hours reading the Bible and theological books. I studied church history and read commentaries to discover what others had learned about the Bible. I learned Greek to understand the New Testament better. After decades of Bible study, I discovered that, for all my biblical knowledge, I was not any relationally closer to Jesus, and I definitely wasn't happier. I knew a lot about Jesus and what he taught. And although I could give biblical explanations for human problems, I still struggled with some of those same problems. With all my biblical knowledge, I found myself hungry for the joy and freedom the Bible described. I discovered that knowledge of the Bible could not give to me what the Bible described.

Because of my love of study and knowledge, I have been involved in adult education for many years. It may be strange for someone engaged in education to question the value of study. Nevertheless, as followers of Jesus, it is important to be aware of what the Bible says about education and the acquisition of knowledge. We live in a day when education is so highly valued that many young people graduate from college with thousands, if not tens of thousands, of dollars of debt. Some young people graduate from high school, even from Christian high schools, with the assumption that they must attend schools of a certain reputation. Students are told that if they get a college education from a prestigious school, they will make a higher income. While in some cases that is true, the implication leads some to believe that anyone who makes more money will be happier. The latter is not necessarily true. If it were, we in the United States—one of the wealthiest nations in the world—should be the happiest, but we often are not. If education could make us happy, that would mean those who have a college degree would be happier and have less problems than those who don't, but we all know that is not necessarily true either.

Solomon had some insight regarding the accumulation of knowledge. In this discussion, I am equating modern society's pursuit of education with what Solomon called the pursuit of wisdom. I recognize that pursuing a formal education is not the same as becoming wise. Many are wise who have never received a formal education. However, I would argue that the intent of formal education is to equip students with skills, knowledge, and wisdom. While educators may disagree on the definition of a wise person, most educators don't intend to produce educated fools. Rather, he or she desires to produce educated and wise students according to his or her definition of educated and wise.

In Ecclesiastes 1:1-18, Solomon describes his approach. He gave himself to the practice of observing how humankind on earth lived, and because of his practice, Solomon became an expert on human behavior. Today we would call him a psychologist, sociologist, and anthropologist, all rolled into one. He observed individual behavior as a psychologist would. He observed social behavior as a sociologist would. And he observed the development of people and societies as an anthropologist would. What he discovered was not encouraging. His conclusion was that the way most people live their lives produces no lasting meaning (Ecclesiastes 1:14). After his study, Solomon drew two conclusions about humans. What is broken cannot be fixed, and he could not count all the problems that he observed (Ecclesiastes 1:15). More than any other ruler, Solomon gave himself over to wisdom in order to observe and interpret human behavior (1:16). His procedure revealed to him that even the acquisition of knowledge, which he used to observe other humans, was itself empty (1:17). In verse eighteen, he made his final conclusion; the acquisition of wisdom and knowledge increased grief and pain in his life. Solomon's words remind us of the saying, "ignorance is bliss." By becoming informed of humankind's situation, Solomon had to find a way to emotionally process that knowledge and live with the consequences.

In Ecclesiastes 1:18, Solomon makes a surprising statement for those of us who give ourselves to the pursuit of wisdom through education. Since the Old Testament almost always refers to "wisdom" in a positive sense, Solomon's conclusion is shocking. When I read it for the first time, I wasn't sure that I agreed with him. Solomon declared that, in much wisdom, there is much grief, and with increased knowledge, comes increased pain. How could Solomon conclude that something so useful as wisdom be the source of pain? Since the acquisition of wisdom is often spoken of so positively, shouldn't it decrease pain? At least that was my assumption. I was prompted to further consider wisdom as it is taught in the Old Testament.

In Exodus 31:3-6, the Spirit of God gave wisdom to build the beautiful articles of the Tabernacle. In this case, the same wisdom—which Solomon declared brought pain—was imparted by the Spirit of God to create a place of worship. According to Deuteronomy 34:9, Joshua was filled with the same wisdom Moses had in order to lead the people of Israel into the Promised Land. The people of Israel recognized the wisdom of Solomon after observing Solomon's wise judgment (1 Kings 3:28). Solomon's wisdom was acknowledged not as the source of his study, but as something God had given to him (1 Kings 4:29-30; 5:12; 10:23-24). Consistently in the Old Testament, true wisdom is associated with God (Psalm 104:24).

When people possess wisdom, their wisdom is recognized as having come from God (Proverbs 2:6). In the Psalms and Proverbs, the fear of the Lord is revealed to be the beginning of wisdom (Psalm 111:10; Proverbs 1:7). Proverbs 1:7 indicates that, as we draw into a closer relationship with God, then our knowledge will increase. Proverbs 4:5 and 4:7 instruct us to obtain wisdom so that our understanding may increase. In Isaiah 11:2, wisdom is identified as one of the characteristics of the Messiah. Throughout the Old Testament, wisdom is to be desired and sought after. However, it is most often acquired relationally or through an impartation more than study alone.

Associated with wisdom is the biblical concept of knowledge. On a number of occasions when wisdom was given, knowledge was given as well (Exodus 31:3; 35:31). This connection confirms that both concepts are linked in the Old Testament. When God confronted Job, he challenged him by asking who darkens his counsel without knowledge, implying that true knowledge comes from a divine source (Job 38:2). In other words, by speaking without knowledge as Job was doing, Job questioned the goodness of God's actions toward Job. After being confronted by God, Job repented of the statements he made without knowledge (Job 42:3). For those who pay attention, all of creation reveals knowledge of God (Psalm 19:2). Those who are foolish actually hate knowledge (Proverbs 1:22, 29). Like wisdom, we are instructed to seek knowledge (Proverbs 23:12).

Furthermore, Scripture warns that a lack of knowledge can lead to difficulty in life. The Israelite people were placed in captivity because of a lack of knowledge (Isaiah 5:13; Hosea 4:6). Not only is humankind instructed to seek knowledge, but Daniel understood that knowledge would increase with study (Daniel 12:4). Through the prophet Hosea's book, the Holy Spirit revealed that knowledge is more important than religious practices (Hosea 6:6). Like wisdom, knowledge comes from God and is to be sought after.

All this information on wisdom and knowledge makes Solomon's statement in Ecclesiastes 1:18 all the more curious. If we are instructed to seek wisdom and knowledge, which comes from God as a blessing and gift, how could the gaining of wisdom cause additional grief? That question revealed a disconnect in my thinking. Based on Proverbs 1:7, my assumption was that increased wisdom and knowledge would provide me a life with less grief and pain, rather than more. That assumption forgot an important fact and warning.

Jeremiah warns us not to glory in the wisdom and knowledge we have attained (Jeremiah 9:23). Jesus praised Father for not revealing the gospel to the wise and educated, but for revealing it to infants instead (Matthew 11:25). If humans use the acquisition of wisdom and knowledge to puff themselves up, then their grief will increase. In fact, this is the warning Paul gave to the Corinthians regarding knowledge. Knowledge puffs up, while love builds up (1 Corinthians 8:1). Paul himself took this warning seriously. He told the Philippians that he considered all the benefits of his education and heritage like trash to be thrown out (Philippians 3:7-11). Paul was an educated man who had an honorable family heritage and the best education of his day, yet he found it lacking in comparison to knowing Jesus.

Nevertheless, the more a person grows in true knowledge and wisdom and simultaneously avoids the pitfall of pride, the more their grief and pain will increase according to Solomon. If a person's wisdom and knowledge are drawing them closer to the heart of God, they will feel more and more the pain of humanity as they see reality from God's perspective. The wise and educated person becomes like a doctor or counselor who must help people deal with and overcome the grief of pain and death. The doctor's knowledge of disease and the human body brings him or her face to face with pain and suffering. The doctor's profession and education bring him or her face to face with pain and death. A counselor's knowledge of psychology and behavioral dysfunction brings him or her into daily work with people who are hurting. Wisdom and knowledge increase grief and pain, just as Solomon said they would.

The more an individual grows to know and love the living God, the more they will have a heart that is similar to God's. In other words, what Father feels, his children will also feel. To put it another way, the Christian will become more and more like Jesus, who was also called a man of sorrows (Isaiah 53:3). Jesus, the man who lived in a closer relationship with God the Father than any other person, the man who walked with more wisdom than any other person who has lived or will live, was called a man of sorrows. Of course, Isaiah's comments were in the context of Jesus bearing the pain of sin for all of humankind, which caused him great sorrow. This particular sorrow is what Jesus saved us from, and it is something we will never have to experience or bear. Yet, as we identify with Jesus, we enter into the fellowship of his suffering (Philippians 3:10). We bear some of the sorrow that Jesus experienced, not the sorrow for our own sin, but the sorrow for the condition in which many people live and feel.

Solomon's words in Ecclesiastes are counterintuitive. He does not mean that the acquisition of wisdom and knowledge are without value, but that they do not produce the value and benefit we first thought they would. I assumed that education and wisdom would provide an easier and more comfortable life for me and my family. I assumed that the acquisition of wisdom and knowledge would lead to the "American Dream." In a limited way, education and wisdom may lead to the American Dream, because those with more education tend to have a higher income. Yet, it does not follow that those who have a higher income will live a happier and more joyful life with fewer problems. They may still get cancer. They may lose their children to a tragic accident. This was Solomon's point—wisdom and knowledge cannot spare us from the trials of living in a fallen and corrupted world.

So, what is the purpose of education? We seek wisdom and knowledge through education in order to make a difference. If we are unaware of the plight of the poor, widows, and orphans in the world and society, then we are also unaware of their pain and suffering. However, once we educate ourselves of their situation, then we have to deal with the knowledge of their plight and also consider what responsibility we may have to provide assistance to them. After World War II, the world remained aghast at the revelation of the death camps located in the German countryside. What shocked the world even more was the realization that the local people must have known something was going on but did little to respond. Several years ago, I began learning more about the human trafficking situation in our country. I learned that Portland, where we were living at the time, is one of the worst cities in the country for human trafficking. I can testify that the knowledge of that situation—running rampant in the world today—caused grief. Grief of which I was unaware until I was educated about the evil of human trafficking. With knowledge, we have a responsibility to pray and consider what we can do to help. Human trafficking is just one of the many social problems we have in the world today.

We all recognize that, as humans, we have a responsibility to do what we can to assist those in need. Solomon's conclusions in Ecclesiastes 1:18 underscore what we already know but sometimes forget. Our increased wisdom and knowledge resulting from education also increases our responsibility to respond morally and appropriately to what we have learned. Knowledge of another's painful situation also increases our own pain.

This leads me to address the current focus on formal education. Genesis 2:9 says that God planted the Garden of Eden with both the tree of life and the tree of the knowledge of good and evil in the center. However, it was the latter that was prohibited, not the former (Genesis 2:17). Have you ever wondered why it was the tree of the knowledge of good and evil that was prohibited and not the tree of life? In our examination of the acquisition of knowledge, it is significant to consider why this was the case. Since God gives only good things, we can safely assume that the prohibition from eating of the tree of knowledge would not have been forever, but access was to be temporarily denied for humankind's protection. Since the increase of knowledge and wisdom led to pain and grief, increasing our knowledge before we were ready would be disastrous rather than beneficial. Our society recognizes this when it puts ratings on movies. We know there are subjects young children should not be exposed to for their own good, because they have not yet reached a reasoning capacity or emotional maturity to handle them. The command against eating from the tree of knowledge was for our protection. However, the liar and murderer, Satan, deceived Eve and convinced Adam to disobey. Their disobedience brought grief, pain, and death into humanity through knowledge for which we were not ready. For this reason, God protected humans from the tree of life so that we would not live eternally in such a painful state. Jesus also implied our limited ability to handle knowledge in John 16:12, when he declared that he had much more to say, but the disciples were not ready. However, the Spirit would come and lead us into all truth. It is the Spirit now, who functions as our tree of the knowledge of good and evil and who gives us the amount of knowledge, revelation, and truth that we can handle in any given moment.

In order for us to handle knowledge, we require intimacy with Father. Human desire for knowledge without intimacy led to isolation, pain, and death—but when we have intimacy, we have the support of a relationship with Father to know how to handle the knowledge and wisdom and apply it correctly without it leading to pride or crushing us with grief. In the Beatitudes, Jesus declared, "Blessed are those who mourn, for they will be comforted" (Matthew 5:4). Later, he called people to himself, saying, "Come to Me, all who are weary and heavy-laden, and I will give you rest" (Matthew 11:28). One of the reasons we mourn and are worn out is because our knowledge is greater than our intimacy with Father can support. What we need may not be more information about Father, but a closer relationship with him.

I believe we have misunderstood the purpose of knowledge. While we may think that increased knowledge and education will lead to a more comfortable life, or the fulfillment of the American Dream, it typically does not. Rather, our increase of knowledge leads to an increase of responsibility. This was Paul's point in Romans 1 and 2. Human knowledge of who God is brought the responsibility for people to love, obey, and honor God. When someone refused to do so, he or she brought condemnation upon his or herself (Romans 1:23-25).

I believe our forefathers had a better understanding of these truths than we do today. They had a very different view of education than we do. The purpose of education today has become primarily vocational. Education has become merely a means to increase our income. We find this in public, private, and even home education. Public schools exist to prepare young people to be adults in our society and join the workforce so that they can lead productive lives. Private Christian educators tell the students' parents that by attending their school, their children will be better prepared for college, get higher test scores, and be taught with Christian values so that they will have a stronger chance of attending a "better" college. Many home school parents educate their children at home so that their children will receive a superior education and maintain Christian values with the goal of preparing for college or a vocation.

However, when schools began in the American colonies, the purpose of education was very different. Boys and girls trained for vocations with their parents or through apprenticeships, but they still went to school so they could learn to read the Bible for themselves. Becoming literate and reading the Bible were important values since the end of the Reformation. Previously, the Roman Catholic Church had not encouraged people to read the Bible, and they even discouraged it until the church council known as Vatican II was held in the early 1960s. Whereas widespread Bible ownership was not even feasible before the 1500s, the invention of the printing press enabled families to own their own copies of the Bible for the first time. Thus, years later, colonial parents desired that their children have a knowledge of God, gained through reading the Bible for themselves.

When Christian children graduate today, they may be prepared for college or work, and we honor those students who have done well in their studies. Nevertheless, one question is curiously absent. They may know who Jesus is, but we often fail to ask whether we have prepared them to respond to the question Jesus asked Peter three times in John 21. Do our well-educated students love Jesus more after their Christian education? They may have increased Bible knowledge, and they may know about Jesus, but do they love him and others more than before? Naturally, public schools would never ask that question and are now legally prohibited from asking it. But private Christian schools often don't ask it either. Something is missing from this picture. Loving Jesus is the question of a lifetime. If our Christian education has not led us into deeper knowledge *and* love of Jesus, what does it matter how well prepared we are for the workforce, or how ready we are for further studies at the college of our choice?

As followers of Jesus, we are here to bring heaven to earth. The Lord's Prayer says, "your kingdom come, your will be done on earth as it is in heaven." What would this look like in the area of education? What would it look like for an elementary school, middle school, high school, or college?

Scripture clearly instructs us to seek wisdom and knowledge, but why are we seeking it? What good will it do for us if it only increases our pride? How could the increase of knowledge lead us into a closer relationship with Jesus? If our children are in school, does our school have a plan for helping our child develop a closer and more intimate relationship with him? As we raise up the next generation, our young people must learn to grow deeper with Jesus. As Christian parents, mentors, caregivers, and family members, we must respond to help them.

Questions for Reflection

1. What motivates you in your pursuit of knowledge, wisdom, and education?
2. How has your increased knowledge also increased difficulty in your life?
3. In what ways has your increased knowledge drawn you into a more intimate relationship with Jesus?

THREE

Entertainment Leaves Us Empty

IN AN AFFLUENT SOCIETY, entertainment and recreation take on significant roles. In those societies where people spend the vast majority of daylight hours as well as their energy to find food for that day, there is not much energy or time left for entertainment. However, as a society develops and becomes more prosperous, individuals no longer have to work such long hours, and thus, there is increased opportunity for free time. In the developed and prosperous world, hobbies, recreation, and entertainment become possible, important, and sought after. We not only ask one another what we do for a living, but we also inquire about one another's hobbies. A number of years ago, after the iPod became popular, it was common for people to ask what songs you had on your iPod. Today, Spotify and other music streaming services are designed to allow you to curate playlists with songs to your liking. Netflix seeks to predict programs that you would like and offers them to you. We ask one another what our favorite television shows or movies are.

Awards are given for popular songs, movies, and television shows. Only in a prosperous society are these things even possible. If someone does not have a hobby, but only works, we consider there to be something missing from that person's life. We even have a proverb for it. All work and no play makes Jack a dull boy. Our affluence has made this value possible for us.

While there is nothing wrong with entertainment and healthy diversions from our daily work schedule, we must recognize that what we do after work and on the weekends does not define our life any more than our vocation defines us and gives us value. However, more and more people begin to live for the "weekend" or for meeting friends after work. We have seen an explosion of technology that provides means of entertainment. We have eighty-inch HD televisions with surround sound systems in our houses to give us an experience closer to what we enjoy in a theater. Some dedicate whole rooms as a home theater so they can watch someone else live a life that often is fictional. From sports to talent shows, we watch others do what we dream about. Each year, enormous amounts of money are spent on movies and computer games that will be viewed or played only a handful of times before becoming dated and boring. Then we must go out and find the next movie or video game that has more realistic graphics. Billion-dollar industries have been developed to satisfy our entertainment requirements. Hence, we should take a moment and pause to reflect on why so many of us give so much of our time and money to these diversions.

For those of us who are of the baby boomer generation, we remember the impact of television. Stories were told and problems resolved in thirty-minute segments. We were thrilled with the two or three channels that we could view on a 19-inch black and white television until the hour came when the test pattern showed up around midnight. For our parents, this was a significant advancement from huddling around the radio to hear the next adventure of their favorite radio program. At the same time, our grandparents shuddered at the violence of the Western movies produced in the 1960s. As we grew up, shades of gray on our televisions were replaced with color.

As baby boomers grew up, the music industry exploded with the arrival of the Beatles on *The Ed Sullivan Show*. Singles on 45 RPM records gave way to albums. Eventually, music became more personal with Sony's Walkman and then digital with iPods. Now we stream music through Bluetooth in our cars and through ear buds or headphones. Digital music gave us the opportunity to have hundreds, if not thousands, of songs at our disposal and available for listening to anywhere and anytime. Now we can develop our own personal playlists. When we are connected to the web, we can stream television, movies, and music.

When *Star Wars* debuted in 1977, we were amazed at what George Lucas accomplished with special effects. Then in the early 1980s, personal computers became available. We wondered why anyone would spend hundreds, or sometimes thousands, of dollars for a machine with a blinking green cursor. Even so, we were mesmerized by games like Pong, displayed on a portable television set. Then the Macintosh appeared with its new technology. Now from our computer, we can fly jets, drive race cars, practice being assassins, or conquer the world as leaders of a historic civilization.

We live in a world where so much of our entertainment is personal. We have personal music, personal playlists, and personal videos, all to be played on our own personal equipment including laptops, tablets, and smart phones. Movies now come with the availability to play on television or be installed on these laptops, tablets, and phones. Today, we can take our entertainment anywhere. And while there is not anything immoral with the explosion and growth of technology, an important question remains. Why has entertainment become so popular and pervasive?

For example, why do we give so much of ourselves to entertainment when there is vast poverty in the world? In 1960, President Kennedy challenged us in his inaugural address: "Ask not what your country can do for you, but what you can do for your country." He probably did not have in mind a nation committed to seeking more and better entertainment choices. In 1960, the world faced serious challenges with whole populations in desperation. Today, even more people are in need than there were sixty years ago. So, why are we dedicated to escaping and fleeing into a virtual entertainment world? Because of technology, we are informed of what is taking place in the world like no other generation. In an instant, we can know what is going on thousands of miles away. On 9/11, we all heard, and in some cases watched before our eyes, as the tragedy unfolded in New York City. That was not possible just a few decades ago. Such real time information takes an emotional toll. We desire to escape from the sheer volume of information and the resulting emotional weight. Entertainment provides us with a means to cope and escape from the pain of daily living — to remove ourselves from the struggles in the world, not to mention the tension in our own daily life.

Twenty years ago, an MD wrote a book called *Margins*, and in this book, the author, Dr. Richard Swenson, explains that with each new advance in technology, our stress level increases. His argument is counter-intuitive. We think that with technological advances, we will have less stress, but he demonstrates that the opposite is true, because expectations rise and become unrealistic. Our family experienced this personally. When we moved to Italy in 1988, we depended upon mail to communicate with friends and family back in the States. Typically, a letter took two weeks to travel to or from the USA. Packages took months to be delivered. One year, we celebrated Christmas in April, because that was when we received some Christmas presents from the States. Several years later, e-mail became feasible. We could send a message back to the States in seconds. Before, we would send a letter and not expect a response for at least a month, probably longer. However, with e-mail, if we had not heard back in twenty-four hours, we felt like we were being neglected. Not only that, but the sheer volume of communication increased. To send an e-mail message cost significantly less than sending a letter. So, of course, we sent and received more messages, all of which required a response.

That was over twenty years ago. Now, we not only have e-mail and phone calls, but social media and text conversations as well. Now, we can have access to our e-mail and social media twenty-four hours a day/seven days a week, as long as we have a cell signal or Wi-Fi connection. Our smart phone will notify us every time a text message or e-mail arrives. We are constantly "connected," and there is an expectation that we must keep up and stay connected through all these means. Such a barrage of information and expectations is emotionally taxing. So, it is not surprising that we retreat into a virtual world where we can rest and regain control.

In a significantly less technological society, Solomon pondered similar entertainment issues. After examining the limitations of wisdom and knowledge, he turned to another extreme. In Ecclesiastes 2:1, Solomon looked at joy. He looked for satisfaction in anything that would cause him happiness, but he discovered that these pursuits left him empty. Remember that Solomon did not condemn these concepts as evil or immoral, but as empty and without lasting value.

The word, "joy," is used in the Old Testament to describe that which causes "rejoicing." It is found in the Old Testament ninety-four times and refers to the emotion of glee. Solomon used this word to describe what brought happiness to his heart. He described the methods he used to lighten his load and bring happiness. Solomon used wine to cheer himself. Wine in the Bible is typically used in the context of celebration, as when Jesus turned water into wine at the wedding in Cana. Wine often accompanied the harvest and celebration of God's provision for a family. We get a glimpse of this in Ruth 3:7 when Boaz laid down with a merry heart after eating and drinking. The same concept is presented again in 1 Samuel 25:36 to describe Nabal's merry condition after shearing his sheep. Today, many look to alcohol and drugs to make their heart merry—not so much to celebrate the good things in their life, but to mask the pain and help them forget their struggle. However, as Solomon found wine to be lacking for lasting joy in celebration, many today find alcohol and drugs to be lacking. Our society has recognized its lack and placed restrictions, both social and legal, to limit usage.

However, Solomon did not stop with the usage of wine, but he looked to accomplishments and acquisitions to bring him joy as well. Solomon built great works, which would have included the temple and his own magnificent palace, along with gardens and vineyards, and they brought him much joy. Today, we would refer to Solomon's experience as "the pride of ownership." It is that feeling of satisfaction we receive when we keep our possessions well maintained, and when we cause our homes and yards to be beautiful. Even so, that feeling—while good and pleasant—does not last through the rigors of life.

Solomon spoke of the acquisition of servants and even concubines, indicating that he also explored sexual pleasure to provide himself with lasting joy. Solomon concluded all this to be empty, and he moved on. Unfortunately, today, people find themselves consumed with sexual addictions and overcome with pornography—and some tragically act out what they've viewed. They discover the bitter truth that such actions, rather than leading them to lasting joy, burden them with shame. Others who have acted upon what they've viewed find themselves identified as sexual offenders for the rest of their lives. Many individuals never succeed to free themselves of such addictions. Rather than finding joy in these actions, they are condemned by society to live the rest of their lives identified by their actions. Solomon labeled such actions as empty and vain. They did not, and could not, give to humankind the desired satisfaction.

Solomon concluded by declaring that he did not deny himself anything his eyes desired. In other words, Solomon had the resources to indulge in anything he wanted. When we consider his statement, many of us realize how dangerous such resources would be for us. Solomon lived a life of worldly pursuit, while declaring that in so doing, he did not abandon his wisdom; nevertheless, he did find his pursuit empty.

While entertainment and technology provide benefits, they do not satisfy in the long run. After the two-hour movie, you still have to face the world and respond to the texts you received while you watched. The problems you faced before the movie have not gone anywhere; they still weigh upon your spirit. At best, entertainment is a temporary relief, but not sustainable. When Solomon explored the possibilities of pleasure, he discovered that, while those pleasures were enjoyable, they were in vain. They were in vain because they could offer no lasting help. Filling up on entertainment is like taking an emotional aspirin. While it provides temporary relief, it never addresses and solves the real problem; it only dulls the pain.

While entertainment might have a positive role in modern society, it is not the solution to what ails us. Entertainment can be useful for connecting with friends who view a movie together and discuss it afterwards. Games can be played together with friends and provide an opportunity for socializing. However, if we seek to address solutions to problems of the human heart, we must look somewhere other than entertainment. If we are using entertainment as a refuge from the pain of modern life, we are asking it to do something beyond its capabilities. Like a drug addict who requires larger doses or more powerful drugs to obtain the same euphoric effect, we will always seek better and more amusing forms of entertainment as we become bored and disillusioned with last year's version—just like when we watch old movies that were so "cutting edge" in their day, but now appear like a visual dinosaur.

Since an escape into entertainment cannot satisfy our needs, we need to make sure it does not become our refuge when we face challenges and disappointments in life. While we may be medicating our pain, entertainment is not a fruitful solution; it is in vain, as Solomon put it. Even worse, when we make it a refuge, we place ourselves in a dependent relationship to that form of entertainment and give up a measure of our personal freedom. We become something similar to a drug addict. Although we may not be physically dependent, we may become emotionally dependent in an unhealthy way that impacts other relationships. We may find ourselves continually choosing to watch television or play a video game rather than interact with our spouse, friends, or children. While there may not be legislation against such behavior, it is not healthy. Rather than seeking an easy route to relieve our pain, we need to seek out the solution that will not only address our pain, but also give us a true solution.

So, what is the role of entertainment? While it cannot offer lasting solutions to our life struggles, it has the role of recreation. It can be useful for resting from the normal stresses of daily living. Hobbies can put us in contact with others of like interest and offer us new opportunities for friendship.

Questions for Reflection

1. What roles do entertainment and hobbies play in your life?
2. What friendships have you seen develop through your hobbies?
3. When you are distraught, what do you do or where do you go for relief?
4. How would you describe a person who makes Jesus their refuge?

FOUR

Money and Possessions Are Given to Bless Others

WHEN I WAS a sophomore in high school, I had speech class. While I don't remember much from that class, other than the embarrassment and anxiety over speaking in front of my peers, I do remember giving one speech. I spoke about how I wanted to become wealthy and enjoy the benefits of wealth. After giving the speech, I recall my teacher's question to me. "Have you considered the headaches that come with wealth?" I hadn't. Actually, I didn't think there were any headaches or responsibilities associated with having great material wealth. From my fifteen-year-old perspective, more money was the solution to all problems. I had watched our family's business go out of existence because of my dad's failing health and the housing downturn of the early 1970s. Money was tight, so I thought that if I had enough money, I could purchase what I wanted. If I could purchase what I wanted, it followed in my thinking that I would be happy. My reasoning went like this. I was happy when I got what I wanted. Therefore, if I could always buy what I wanted, then I would always be happy. In other words, I had fully committed my thinking to the American Dream! Actually, I had allowed a lie to enter into my thinking because of my family's financial difficulties. The lie was that money would make me happy.

Solomon, who actually had enough wealth to do whatever he wanted, experienced what I dreamt of as a fifteen-year-old. However, his conclusions were very different from my assumptions. In Ecclesiastes 5, he wrote of what he learned by pursuing and enjoying material wealth. His words may surprise those of us who have given ourselves to believing in what has been called the American Dream. Many of us assume that if we have a certain level of income, own our own home, and have some left over for recreation, then we will be happy. The path to the American Dream has classically been called hard work. And before we consider Solomon's observations, it would be helpful to see how money is presented in other areas of the Bible.

In the Old Testament, the most common word for money is "silver." In our English versions, sometimes the word is translated as "silver," and at other times as "money." Typically, it is translated as "silver" when the word is used in conjunction with the word "gold." Although the Hebrew word for silver was also used in the broader sense as "money," it is clear that gold was also used as a form of money. But the word for "gold" is never translated as "money," while "silver" is. In the ancient world, silver became a means of purchasing goods and services. In the Old Testament, it was the usual standard of trade.

Even in our nation, gold was for many years the foundation for our currency. Gold was finally removed as a standard for our currency under President Nixon on August 15, 1971. On the same night, he imposed a wage and price freeze. In other words, since the 1970s, the money we work hard for has had absolutely no backing except the word of our government. Technically, it is called "fiat money," meaning it is declared to be money.

It is somewhat ironic that many Americans work so hard for something that has such little real value. It reminds us of the message to the Israelites in Isaiah 44. Isaiah told them how foolish it was for them to cut down a tree and use only part of it for warmth and to cook their food—while making the rest of it an idol. Our currency, which is also made from trees, can be used for good, but it is foolish for us to think that the acquisition of money is the purpose of our life or to think that having money will deliver us from life's problems (Isaiah 44:14-17).

According to Numbers 3, money was used for the purpose of redemption. Every firstborn man or animal had to be redeemed. In the case of Israel, each Levite male redeemed one male firstborn Israelite from the other tribes. However, at the time, there were two hundred and seventy-three more Israelite firstborn males than there were male Levites. The two hundred and seventy-three remaining firstborn were redeemed with five shekels of silver each (Numbers 3:40-51). Under the law, men could be redeemed with money.

However, the Israelites were enslaved by being conquered so that Isaiah would prophecy that they were sold for nothing and redeemed without money (Isaiah 52:3). Isaiah's words looked forward to the redemption that Jesus accomplished without money, but with his blood. In Isaiah 55, the prophet questioned the misuse of money, asking why they spent their money and labor on efforts that do not satisfy (Isaiah 55:2). In so doing, the prophet called them to come to the Lord to receive joy and satisfaction that does not cost money (Isaiah 55:1). In Isaiah, we begin to see repeated the point that Solomon made in Ecclesiastes—that money does not satisfy. Therefore, we should not live for it.

In the New Testament, the word for money is translated as either "mammon" (Matthew 6:24), which came from the Babylonian language and means "confidence," or the Greek word for "silver" (Matthew 25:18). On a few occasions, the Greek word for "riches" is translated as "money" (Acts 24:26). The use of the word "silver" maintained the Old Testament concept equating silver with money. In the Gospels, the dangers of desiring money are described. The Pharisees, who were lovers of money, ridiculed Jesus when he taught that you could not serve both God and money (Luke 16:13-14). Jesus' instruction was that we were to invest our treasure (money) in heaven where it will be safe, rather than on earth where we can lose it (Matthew 6:20-24). In the Parable of the Unrighteous Servant, Jesus made the point that, rather than worshiping money, we are to use it to bless others for the kingdom of God. How we use money will determine whether we are entrusted with kingdom riches (Luke 16:1-11). This is a parable that many people struggle to understand, because Jesus praises an unrighteous and dishonest servant. We wonder how Jesus could praise someone who benefited from dishonesty. However, he does not praise him for dishonesty, but because he used his position to secure his future. As followers of Jesus, we are to do the same. This was the point at the end of the parable. We are to use earthly wealth and invest it for eternal purposes. This is the same point Jesus made in Matthew 6. Jesus said we should not invest in worldly things, as they will be lost. Rather, we are to invest in heavenly things that will never be lost.

Those who failed to follow Jesus' instruction and gave themselves to loving money were consistently shown to be foolish. Judas agreed to betray Jesus for money (Luke 22:3-5), because he was a thief who stole money from Jesus and the other disciples (John 12:5-6). Simon desired to purchase the ability to bestow the Holy Spirit on others, but Peter rebuked him because of his desire to purchase the gift of God with money (Acts 8:18-20). To Timothy, Paul warned that the love of money (silver) leads to all sorts of evil (1 Timothy 6:10). The New Testament points out that while money can be used for good, the love of it always leads to evil and is a characteristic of the ungodly (2 Timothy 3:2). Contrasted with the love of money is the concept of being content with what we have (Hebrews 13:5). The follower of Jesus can avoid the love of money and be content because of the promise Father has given—that he will never leave us nor forsake us. When we have the promise of Father to take care of us, there is no need to be tempted by the love of money. With this biblical overview of money, we can take a look at Solomon's instruction.

In Ecclesiastes 5:10-12, Solomon describes the problems that accompany the love of money. He points out that consumption rises with income. In verse 10, he declares that the one who loves money will never be satisfied with it. Famous businessman and philanthropist, John D. Rockefeller was asked, "How much money is enough?" He responded, "Just a little more." His response reflects the point that Solomon made and the lie that has taken root in many Americans. Although Rockefeller was one of the richest men in American history, he quite likely was not one who loved wealth. He once was quoted as saying he never intended to become wealthy, but to build. Nevertheless, his quote about a little more money reflects Solomon's wise statement that money can never satisfy the human heart. Those who love money only end up desiring more and waste their life in a vain effort to satisfy their own desires.

Solomon's words remind us of an important truth. Because we are created in the image of God, we can never be satisfied by what is of this world. We can only be satisfied by what satisfies our heavenly Father. Our Father has no need for material things; therefore, they cannot satisfy him. As Father uses material things to bless his children, we use material wealth to meet both our needs and to bless others. We do have need of material things, but they still cannot satisfy us. We must recognize that there is a difference between having a physical need met and feeling satisfied.

As a person's wealth increases, the drain on their wealth also tends to increase. Another way to express this is that as our income rises, our desires for more seem to increase as well. What is also curious is that our desires often rise faster than our income does. We experience an increase in wealth, so we begin to imagine all the ways we could spend it. They are all desirable, but we can only spend our wealth once, so we remain disappointed in all the areas where we could not spend our money. Or, we can consider many who have won the lottery. Winners of the lottery discover that their winnings can be gone in a very short period of time. People whom they have never met come calling and asking them for financial help. Soon, those who do not practice wise financial planning find that their new wealth is all gone, and in many cases, they are worse off financially than they were before they won the lottery. The National Endowment for Financial Education discovered that 70% of lottery winners go broke in a few years. Some do not manage their new personal spending well, confirming what Solomon observed.

Solomon also prophesied what Jesus would teach in the Sermon on the Mount. Everything we gain on earth will eventually be sacrificed. In Ecclesiastes 5:13, Solomon made additional observations. He first noted the problem with hording. Solomon observed individuals who held on to their wealth to their own detriment. We find examples of this in the Bible. Nabal, whose shepherds and flocks David had protected, refused to give assistance to David. His selfishness almost resulted in David's coming and taking his life, except that Nabal's wife, Abigail, wisely intervened and did what her husband should have done—saving the household from disaster. Nevertheless, Nabal fell dead when he heard what had happened (1 Samuel 25:2-38). Interestingly, in Hebrew, Nabal means "fool." He tried to hang onto his wealth, but it led to his own demise.

In the New Testament, the rich young ruler was instructed by Jesus to give away his wealth and follow Jesus, but he could not part with his riches. Luke recorded that the young man, loved by Jesus, went away sad. He had his wealth, but it became the reason for his sadness and prevented him from experiencing true life (Luke 18:18-23).

In 1906, Fredrick Gates warned John D. Rockefeller that his fortune was growing so fast that if he did not disperse it, it would ruin him and his family. Rockefeller wisely accepted his friend's advice and increased his philanthropic work. I wonder if Gates was familiar with Solomon's warning in Ecclesiastes 5:13. Rockefeller went on to give away over five hundred and fifty million dollars over the course of the last thirty years of his life. Further, that sum was not calculated in today's dollars, but with the figures applicable before 1937 when he died.

John D. Rockefeller is remembered for giving to those in need. Rockefeller left a fortune to his family who, over the last seventy years, has continued to advance his philanthropic works. He also dedicated a significant portion of his wealth to education. Through his giving, he turned a small Baptist college in Chicago into a well-known University, known today as the University of Chicago. Although extremely wealthy, individuals like Rockefeller remind us what Solomon taught in Ecclesiastes.

The main point Solomon makes about wealth is that we must learn to enjoy what we have received from God. What we have will never satisfy our deeper desires, but if we learn to enjoy what we have, then we will find contentment. Solomon made an important observation. Our joy does not come from what we have, but it comes from our relationship with the living God, who has become our Father through faith in Jesus.

The apostle Paul learned the same lesson to which Solomon referred. In fact, I believe we find a progression in Paul's growth. When Paul wrote to Timothy in

Ephesus, he declared to him that godliness with contentment is great gain. Paul explained that if we have both food and clothing, then we will be content. Paul's point is that when we have a right relationship with Father (godliness), then we need very little to be content—only food and clothing (1 Timothy 6:7-8). Paul went on to warn those who desired to be rich, informing them that their desires would lead them into a snare. Most of us living in the United States or other developed countries would find it difficult to be content with only food and clothing; however, this is how Jesus lived. He had no home; he had no consistent income. His brothers did not believe in him. In other words, Paul exhorted Timothy to live like Jesus and live for the kingdom, not for the accumulation of things in this world.

What is interesting is that a few years later, Paul wrote another letter; this time to the Philippians. In that letter, Paul went even further. While under house arrest, Paul declared to the Philippians that he had learned to be content in all situations—including those situations where even his basic needs were not met (Philippians 4:11-13). Paul had grown in maturity between the time he wrote 1 Timothy and Philippians. To Timothy, he implied that food and clothing were necessary for contentment, but to the Philippians, he stated that one could be content even when the basic needs of life were lacking. That is extraordinary.

How is it possible? Paul learned the kingdom principle that contentment does not come from what we have and does not flee when we do not have our physical needs met. When we have the Spirit of God dwelling with us, our bodies may have need, but our spirits have more than they need because of God's presence with us.

We must understand that our money and possessions are tools to expand the kingdom of God, not a means to make us happy. The world lies to us and tells us we need material things, money, and possessions to be content. They are not given for us to be happy, because we don't need them for contentment or happiness. When our youngest son, Brian, went on a mission trip to India, he made an astute observation. His team primarily worked with children, and Brian noted that the children who had little—much less than he did—were happy.

Our American Dream culture has lied to us. We have bought into the lie that we need a certain number of things to be content and happy: an education, a certain level of income, a regular job that provides income, friends, hobbies, functioning cars, a comfortable home, etc. However, Jesus, Paul, and some children from India indicate that this belief is a lie. It is merely what our culture says, not what God has decreed.

Rather than being necessary for happiness, our money and possessions are meant to be a blessing for others. If we have been blessed with wealth, then we have the responsibility to utilize that wealth to bless others. When a rich man, Zacchaeus, came to the truth, he gave half of his wealth to the poor (Luke 19:8). While the previously mentioned rich young ruler left Jesus sad, Zacchaeus, a redeemed greedy and immoral tax-collector, was filled with joy. He was joyful, not so much because he gave his wealth away, but because he had come to know Jesus. Giving away his wealth was the natural result of his coming to know Jesus. He no longer needed all that money to be happy.

This was Jesus' point when he taught on wealth in the Sermon on the Mount. He gave the disciples a series of negative commands to correct what they were currently doing. In Matthew 6:19-20, he told them to stop laying up for themselves treasures on earth, but to lay up treasure in heaven. Laying up treasures for ourselves on earth is normal human behavior; yet, Jesus told his disciples to stop. In Matthew 6:25, Jesus gave his conclusion. They were to stop being anxious about their lives. When contentment and hope are tied to money and earthly treasures, then anxiety is the only result, because men will live in fear of losing them. However, there was no need to be anxious because Father would take care of them. This is the secret of contentment. To the extent we are confident that Father will take care of our needs, then we are free to use our money and possessions to assist those who have greater needs than we do. When we begin to doubt Father's goodness and generosity, then we pull back and believe the lie that we need our money and possessions to meet our needs and keep us happy.

In other words, Jesus calls us to become children who inherit the kingdom of heaven. Children of a loving and good father do not worry about their food, clothing, shelter, or future. This is the picture Jesus gives to us in the Sermon on the Mount. He described a life of freedom from anxiety, because all of our needs will be met. Even on those occasions when we may experience temporary lack, he is with us and will give us the joy of his presence with us.

By his teaching, Jesus does not mean that we are not

to work hard. No one worked harder than Jesus and the apostles. Jesus did not receive a salary for being the world's Savior. The apostles did not receive a salary for proclaiming the truth, although Paul argued strongly that they should be provided for. Rather, we are to work hard to expand the kingdom, not our bank accounts. This is the thing. God may provide for his children through normal means such as jobs and businesses. Or, he may provide through unusual means. In either case, we must keep our focus on the kingdom of heaven. This is the message Jesus gave to his disciples in Matthew 6.

We have been deceived to think that work is all about income. We believe the lie that we are to work to make money and that money will make us content. Then we also attach our worth to how much income we have. Someone whose income is one hundred thousand dollars is considered more valuable than someone whose income is twenty thousand dollars. Jesus, the apostles, and countless others who have given their life for the kingdom prove that to be a lie. Income is a byproduct. We work because we are created to do so, in order to promote the kingdom.

All of us have been given wealth. Some of our wealth is material—money and possessions—but we have other forms as well. We all have the same amount of time—one hundred sixty-eight hours every week. We have all been given gifts from the Holy Spirit, to go along with the natural talents given to us at birth. It is a lie that any of us are poor! Rather the question is, how will we each use our wealth for the kingdom?

What lies have we believed regarding our money and possessions? What is keeping us from experiencing what

Paul declared—that, whether in abundance or lack and whether satisfied or hungry, he had learned to be content? If we cannot honestly say the same thing, then we have believed lies about our money and possessions. We must address those lies, confront them, repent from them, leave them at the foot of the cross, and receive the better gift from the hand of Jesus.

Questions for Reflection

1. How would you describe your view of money and possessions?
2. How attached is your income level to your contentment and how you see yourself?
3. In what ways can your present wealth, possessions, and income be used as a blessing for those in need?

FIVE

The Pursuit of Jesus is Worth Everything

AS A CHILD, I looked forward to Christmas. In the fall—still weeks before the big day—I poured over the Christmas catalogs that came in the mail. I imagined playing with the various toys pictured and told my parents about the ones I wanted. On Christmas morning, I always awoke early, thrilled to see what presents awaited me. My parents never seemed to wake up soon enough for me, and they would not let me go out into the living room without them either. Now I know why. Their joy was experiencing the joy my sister and I had with the sight of the presents positioned around the tree. Both of my parents grew up during the Great Depression. While they both had all their needs met, Christmas was not always known for abundance. What they had lacked, they made sure my sister and I enjoyed and rejoiced themselves.

Even though Christmas was a day of great joy spent with toys, grandparents, and cousins, the day after Christmas was a downer because I realized a whole year would have to go by until the next Christmas. Looking back, I am sad to realize that as a young boy, I was so focused on the joy of one day and often missed the potential joy of so many other days. However, sometime in January, after I went back to school, the reality of routine settled in, and the joy of Christmas faded until the next fall when the catalogs came again.

Jesus revealed to his disciples a joy that endures a lifetime. The joy of Jesus had a different foundation than the joy I experienced each Christmas during my childhood. Ironically, one of the most joy-filled books in the New Testament, Philippians, was written by a man under house arrest, the apostle Paul. After giving a world class description of Jesus in chapter 2, Paul went on to emphasize joy and the act of rejoicing in the final two chapters.

Initially, it might seem strange that Paul commanded the Philippians to rejoice in the Lord and then immediately warned them about those who oppose the gospel with false religion. It seems like an odd contrast. That contrast invites us to look more deeply into how Jesus defined joy. The world identifies joy and rejoicing in much the same way I did as a young boy. When good things happen to us, we rejoice. However, the world questions the reason for rejoicing when we face conflict and struggle. Nevertheless, conflict was the situation in which Paul told the Philippians to rejoice. They faced suffering from those who did not proclaim the truth; yet, Paul instructed them to rejoice in the Lord. Paul understood that false religion was connected to the world's values; therefore, he instructed the believers to make sure their joy was in the right place.

Paul's instruction leads us to ask why they were to

rejoice in the midst of conflict. The word, "rejoice," throughout the New Testament, is consistently linked to Jesus. The only times it does not have any connection with Jesus is when it is used as a greeting, as in "hail." Those who loved Jesus rejoiced in him and his salvation. Those who opposed Jesus rejoiced in his death (John 16:20) or the demise of his servants (Revelation 11:10). At Jesus' birth, there was rejoicing (Matthew 2:10; Luke 1:14). Salvation and the knowledge of having eternal life were reasons for rejoicing (Matthew 5:12; 18:13). Jesus warned his followers not to rejoice in their spiritual power and authority, but because they had eternal life (Luke 10:20). Jesus declared that even Abraham rejoiced at seeing his day (John 8:56). Jesus' comment regarding Abraham indicates that throughout history, Jesus has been the reason for great joy.

Not only is the verb "rejoice" consistently related to Jesus, but so is the noun "joy." John the Baptist declared that it was his great joy to be the friend of the bridegroom (John 3:29). When just one person repents and follows Jesus, there is great joy in heaven (Luke 15:7, 10). Jesus taught his disciples so that his joy would be in them (John 15:11). Afterwards, he told them that they had great authority and freedom in prayer. They would ask and receive so that their joy would be made full (John 16:24). The women departed from Jesus' empty tomb with great joy (Matthew 28:8). After Jesus ascended into heaven, the disciples returned to Jerusalem with great joy (Luke 24:52). When Paul and Barnabas proclaimed Jesus to the Gentiles in Iconium, the believers were filled with joy and the Holy Spirit (Acts 13:52). One of the foundational principles of the kingdom is joy along with peace in the

Holy Spirit (Romans 14:17). It should not surprise us that joy, as well as peace, are consistently linked to the Holy Spirit, since Paul taught that these are two of the nine fruits of the Spirit (Galatians 5:22-23).

In contrast to the world's view of joy, Jesus' disciples even rejoiced when facing difficulty (Acts 5:41). After being beaten for preaching and disregarding the Jews' command to stop, the disciples rejoiced because they were considered worthy to suffer for Jesus' name. Even in sorrow, followers of Jesus can rejoice (2 Corinthians 6:10). Paul rejoiced when he made sacrifices for the increase of the faith of the Philippians (Philippians 2:17). He instructed the Colossians to rejoice in his sufferings for them (Colossians 1:24). To the Corinthians, Paul affirmed that he was joyful in the midst of tribulation (2 Corinthians 7:4). In the midst of their afflictions, the Macedonian Christians gave to their brothers and sisters in Jerusalem with great joy (2 Corinthians 8:2). Peter informed his readers that they were to rejoice because they shared in Jesus' sufferings (1 Peter 4:13).

According to *Merriam Webster*, the opposite of the verb "to rejoice" is "to be displeased." However, if we can rejoice in the midst of sorrow, which is displeasing, how can displeasure be the opposite of rejoicing? *Webster's Dictionary* reflects the world's view, which equates rejoicing with an emotion, but biblically, rejoicing must be more than that. Since, in the New Testament, rejoicing for the believer is always linked to Jesus, the action of rejoicing must be a decision to hope and believe in the promises of Jesus regardless of circumstances. Our rejoicing is independent from our earthly situation, as Jesus told his disciples to rejoice because their names were written in the book of life, not because they had authority and success on earth. In Luke 10, when the seventy returned with stories of great victory over disease and demons, Jesus rejoiced with them but also cautioned them not to rejoice for the reason that they had authority over spirits (Luke 10:17-20).

Why did Jesus give them this instruction? The joy of having authority over spirits is connected to the world and passes away, while having your name written in heaven is connected to heaven and will never pass away. We are to make the focus of our joy on heaven and the eternal, not on earth and the temporal.

The biblical view of joy and rejoicing reveals how different the kingdom of God is from the world. The child of our Father in heaven does not need pleasant circumstances to be joyful, nor does tribulation hinder their rejoicing. Day in and day out, the child lives with great joy, because their identity and treasure are located in heaven and not on earth. On a personal level, joy also reveals to me how much the world, and not the kingdom of God, has impacted my life. Some have concluded that having heaven-related joy causes followers of Jesus to be disconnected from the problems of the world. But rather, just the opposite is true. Since, like Jesus, his followers do not depend upon pleasant circumstances for their joy, they are free to focus their energies on the needs of others.

During the majority of our first four years working as missionaries in Italy, we lacked significant financial support. I found this situation discouraging, and it often produced anxiety. However, during our final seven years living overseas, we were fully supported, and I was more relaxed as well as emotionally at peace. My heart condition revealed how much the world's values still had a grip on my life. Why was my joy dependent on my finances? If my name is written in heaven and I am a child of the king, why do I rejoice when I am well off and become disheartened when I have a perceived need? Actually, neither circumstance should impact my joy. The truth is my behavior reflects more of the world than heaven. The world rejoices when good things happen and becomes discouraged when they don't. If that is how I live, how can I reveal to the world that following Jesus is transformational in my life?

Consider Jesus' words in Luke 10 about rejoicing because our names are written in heaven. Also consider what Paul wrote to the Corinthians about gold, silver, wood, hay, and stubble. Paul told the Corinthians that some of their works will endure the fire of testing, while others will be burned up (1 Corinthians 3:12-15). Paul's instruction raised a question for me. Which of my/our works will remain, and which ones will be destroyed? Generally, I think it safe to assume that those works which we have done under the power of the Holy Spirit will remain, while those done in our own strength will be destroyed. Jesus gave us at least one glimpse of what it looks like to live in the Spirit. During his teaching in the Sermon on the Mount, he asked his disciples what reward they will receive if they only love those who love them, or if they only greet their brothers—because even those without God do that. In other words, anyone in their own power can love those who love them. It requires no supernatural power to greet one's own brothers and sisters. Rather, Jesus commanded his disciples to love even their enemies (Matthew 5:43-48). Implied in Jesus' words is the reality that only in the power of the Spirit can we truly love our enemies, because that action runs contrary to our flesh. So, how does this relate to rejoicing?

What type of rejoicing requires supernatural power, and what type of rejoicing can be done in the flesh? When the disciples rejoiced after being beaten because it linked them to Jesus, they did so with supernatural power, because no one else would or could do that. On the other hand, suppose someone receives recognition at work, along with a promotion. Even those without God will rejoice at that. It takes no supernatural power to rejoice in positive circumstances, even though doing so honors God and is good. However, suppose someone is treated unjustly at work, didn't get a deserved promotion, or is laid off. The godless don't typically rejoice in those situations, but the lover of Jesus can. This doesn't mean that we rejoice because of the adversity, or worse, conclude that the adversity came from our Father in order to teach us a lesson. Rather, we rejoice because, in spite of the difficulty, we affirm that the heavenly reality of our relationship with Father has not changed. In so doing, we reveal the power of the kingdom of God. Despite our circumstances, we know that our names are written in heaven, and that truth has not changed if we get a promotion or if we are laid off. In each situation, we have equal reason to rejoice. Receiving a promotion or being laid off is a temporary occurrence that will not last. We do not rejoice in circumstances, but in the reality of the divine promise of eternal life in Jesus. When the world sees us rejoicing over eternal realities in the midst of temporal difficulties, they must wonder why. When other believers see us rejoicing in the midst of difficulty, they are encouraged to do the same in their time of difficulty. On the other hand, when the world sees us rejoice only in temporal blessings and become discouraged and downcast in difficulty, they have to wonder what benefit there is in following Jesus and having the Holy Spirit dwell within, because that is exactly the same way they live.

Now, if you will let me speculate a bit. We know that our difficulties are opportunities to build faith in Jesus and reveal God's kingdom on earth. Paul taught that some of our works will be considered gold and silver surviving the fire of testing. However, other works will be wood, hay, and stubble being burned up and destroyed. The question is, what is the difference between the two? What if loving our enemies, which the godless often won't do, forgiving those who hurt us, which the godless often won't do, and rejoicing in the midst of tribulation, again what the godless often will not do, are our primary opportunities to produce kingdom gold while we dwell on this earth? This is a speculation, and I cannot prove this from Scripture, other than Jesus' command to rejoice in our eternal life and not in our earthly spiritual authority. But I do believe it is worth pondering.

This is why I believe we need to find ways to build intentional worship into our lives every day and often, if not always, throughout the day. We need to build the practice of worship and praise, not based on our circumstances, but based on God's promises to us. I have not arrived. Often, I will be at work and realize I have not thought about Jesus for hours. If I have not thought about Jesus, then I clearly have not prayed or communed with him either.

There is a very important reason for us to practice joy

and worship continually in our lives—we are at war. We battle the spiritual authorities in the world (Ephesians 6:12). Many people follow religious systems, and many Christians have been deceived into following religious and theological systems that claim to be biblically true but have added the traditions of humans to the gospel. This is what Paul warned the Philippians about. Christians were going around teaching believers that they had to follow the Jewish religious traditions in order to know Jesus. Paul declared that this was a false gospel.

If Paul had been a typical man of the world, maybe even a typical Christian, he would have rejoiced in who he was and what he had accomplished. No one had a higher religious pedigree than Paul. He was born into the right Jewish tradition, respected and envied throughout the Jewish world. He held an education that few of his day had the privilege of receiving. Yet, he considered all those privileges nothing in comparison to knowing Jesus. How he considered what he received is significant for us to consider, particularly those of us who are tempted to be joyful in pleasant circumstances and disheartened in tribulation.

The New Testament consistently presents Jesus as worth giving up everything for. Jesus himself described the kingdom's value through telling the parables of the field and the pearl. When a man found a treasure buried in a field, he joyfully liquidated all he had so he could purchase the field and obtain the treasure. When the merchant discovered a priceless pearl, he joyfully sold all of his assets. He emptied his bank account and liquidated his investments so that he could purchase that one pearl (Matthew 13:44-46). Jesus told his disciples that in comparison to their love for him, their affections for everything else would appear as hate (Luke 14:26-27). In other words, to the world, we lovers of Jesus will appear odd. We will not fit in the world, which means we should not be surprised when we feel excluded or feel like misfits. Or to put it another way, if we are comfortable in the world, maybe we should ask why.

Peter grasped the value of Jesus. After Jesus fed the five thousand and they left because his teaching was hard, Jesus turned to his disciples and asked them if they were going to leave as well. Peter answered for them all. Peter affirmed that Jesus was the only one who had the words of eternal life (John 6:66-69). Peter understood that although Jesus taught things that were difficult to understand and accept, he also was the only one who offered new life. Peter and the other disciples were willing to accept what they struggled to understand in order to gain what they couldn't receive from anyone else.

The rich young ruler instructs us on the futility of trying to reconcile the world with the kingdom. He tried to gain eternal life and hang onto his worldly wealth. He ended up leaving Jesus in sadness. In a way, the rich young ruler missed the point. He came to Jesus seeking eternal life, but he apparently wasn't interested in following or knowing Jesus. He wanted something from Jesus; he apparently didn't want Jesus. It is my suspicion that many Christians live just like him. I say this because I lived like him and am now in the process of unlearning that perspective. Years ago, someone told me that many evangelical Christians worship the Bible more than God. As a lover of the Bible, I was offended. But now, as I look back at my attitude as a student at San Jose State, later at

Denver Seminary, and then as a missionary, I confess I was more concerned about "right doctrine" than I was about my Father's heart revealed through Jesus. In other words, I resembled the rich young ruler. In many ways, I was like a Christian Pharisee. I don't think it is coincidence that the Holy Spirit led Luke to write of the rich young ruler, a good man in the world's eyes, but not yet ready for the kingdom. Then, the Spirit led Luke to contrast the young man with another rich man, Zacchaeus, who was not worthy of eternal life in the world's eyes. Notice the difference between Zacchaeus and the rich young ruler. Zacchaeus climbed that Sycamore tree to see Jesus. Jesus was his focus, not what Jesus had to offer. The rich young ruler wanted eternal life and gave Jesus his spiritual resume to show he deserved it. When Jesus told Zacchaeus that he would be dining with him, Zacchaeus was thrilled. When Jesus told the rich young ruler to sacrifice everything to follow him, the young ruler was sad. Jesus declared that, without God's intervention, it is impossible for a rich man to enter the kingdom. On the other hand, Zacchaeus was so thankful that Jesus came into his house, he gave away his fortune. Jesus declared that Zacchaeus, the tax collector, had found salvation, while the rich young ruler provoked Jesus' comment on how difficult it is for the rich to enter the kingdom. Zacchaeus pursued Jesus and not only got what he desired, but he also got what the rich young ruler sought, eternal life. Once Zacchaeus found Jesus, his fortune no longer had any value to him. On the other hand, the rich young ruler approached Jesus to get eternal life and walked away with neither eternal life, nor salvation.

The rich young ruler was like some religious people

who focus on the pursuit of religious works and Bible study, but subtly neglect Jesus. However, the lover of Jesus discovers that his pursuit of Jesus simply gives him eternal life as a bonus. The lover of Jesus pursues Jesus and is thrilled with whatever life Jesus chooses to bestow upon him, because Jesus is his reward.

In 1980, a movie came out called *Little Lord Fauntleroy*. It was about a little American boy, Cedric or Ceddie, and his aristocratic English grandfather, the Earl of Dorincourt. At the beginning of the movie, it was believed that Ceddie was the last surviving heir to his grandfather. He was brought from America to England and began to learn what it meant to be an Earl. Actually, it was Ceddie who taught his grandfather what it meant to be an Earl, but that is another story. At a certain point, there entered another boy whose mother claimed that he was Ceddie's older cousin. This boy's mother, who had been married to Ceddie's uncle, claimed her son was the legitimate heir. When the grandfather told Ceddie that he was not to be the Earl, Ceddie was not saddened by the loss of the title, but was gripped with fear that he would no longer be his grandfather's little boy. It was the relationship with his grandfather that little Ceddie treasured, not the title or the benefits of that title. My friends, knowing Jesus is our great treasure, much more so than the blessings he gives to us, the greatest of which is eternal life. Eternal life is only joyful because it is lived out in the presence of Jesus and our Father in heaven. Have you ever considered the possibility that the only difference between heaven and hell is the presence of Jesus and Father? Without Jesus and our heavenly Father, eternal life would be hell. To put it another way, heaven is not primarily geographical, but relational. I do not mean to say that heaven is not a place, because it is where God dwells. However, when Satan entered God's presence in the first couple chapters of Job, it was not heaven for him, because his relationship with God had been broken. Yet, when a child of God enters into that same place, it is heaven because of the relationship the child has with Father God.

I believe the apostle Paul grasped this concept. That is why he spoke so disparagingly of his achievements and heritage. What is interesting is that Paul would only use his heritage when it benefited the kingdom. Even at Philippi, he used his Roman citizenship to promote and protect the church. After the Philippian magistrates falsely arrested and beat Paul and Silas, Paul made them publicly escort them out of jail and acknowledge their mistreatment. Paul's actions served to protect the fledgling church that was located in Philippi. When Paul was arrested and about to be beaten by the Roman centurion in Jerusalem, he revealed that he was a Roman citizen. Roman beatings could kill the victim, but the Holy Spirit revealed to Paul that he would go to Rome, so he used his citizenship to possibly preserve his life and preserve his future ministry in Rome.

Nevertheless, Paul's accomplishments were not a source of joy for him. They were mere facts of his background, only to be used to promote Jesus. We are to live in the same manner. All that we are and all that we have been entrusted with are nothing more than resources to be used for the expansion of Jesus' kingdom. Furthermore, this is wise living, because all of our earthly resources are temporary, but Jesus and his kingdom are eternal. We must be vigilant not to fall for the lies of the world, which entice us to try to get the best the world has to offer and still get the kingdom.

However, so we don't assume that following Jesus is all sacrifice and not blessing, Jesus himself reminded Peter and the other disciples that even though they had given up everything to follow him, he would give back much more both in this age as well as in the age to come (Luke 18:28-30). In other words, agree with the words of martyred missionary Jim Elliot, that we sacrifice what we cannot keep, but we receive what we cannot lose. For, if Jesus gives us something, who can take it away from us? However, if we gain something ourselves, we live in fear that someone can take it from us or that we will lose. Even in our sacrifice for Jesus, we gain—because that is the way of the kingdom.

A mind set on earthly things is our enemy (Philippians 3:12-21). That means our big battle is overcoming the world's values and the world's assumptions. We must learn to live according to God's promises and not according to appearances. It means living according to the promises and prophecies that we have received. Like Paul, we run toward the prize of reaching life's finish line, our destiny in Jesus. A number of times in his writings, Paul referred to running a race. This would have made sense to the Greek mindset that was accustomed to athletic games which included running. Paul emphasizes how important it is to keep the goal or finish line in mind. Several years ago, I ran in the Helvetia Half Marathon in Hillsboro, Oregon—thirteen point one miles. My goal was to run the race at a pace a little faster than an eight-minute mile pace, or to finish the race in under an hour and forty-five minutes. Fortunately, the race had pacers who ran with helium-filled balloons attached to them so that you could see them. Since there were so many racers, I could not get up with the eight-minute mile pacer, so I began with the eight-and-a-half-minute mile pacer. I realized that, since I was starting after the eight-minute mile pacer, if I could catch her by the end of the race, then I would have accomplished my goal and would have run under one hour and forty-five minutes. At the seven-and-a-half-mile point, I reached the highest elevation of the race and could see far ahead. That was when I saw my goal, the balloons of the eight-minute mile pacer. For the rest of the race, I kept her in my sight, running to catch up to her. At twelve and a half miles, less than a mile from the finish line, I caught and passed her. As I did, she encouraged me to keep going and finish under an hour and forty-five. I did, finishing a bit under one hour and forty-four minutes.

On the other hand, several years after I ran that half marathon, I ran in a five-kilometer race—just three point one miles. My goal was to run it under twenty minutes. When I started, I had a glitch with my watch, so I didn't have an accurate time of when I began. When I finished, I knew I was close to twenty minutes. When the results came, I finished at twenty minutes and two seconds. Two seconds over twenty minutes, I had missed my goal. If I had a clear idea of my goal as I got close to the finish line, I believe I could have cut two or three seconds off my time. As we run the race of life, we must keep Jesus firmly in our sight, because he is our goal; otherwise, we can become distracted and miss our goal. The purpose of our life is to become like him.

Like Paul, the saints of the Old Testament kept their

destiny in mind, and it carried them through the tribulations of their lives. Consider Abraham and Sarah. When they were already old, God told Abraham that his descendants would be as many as the stars in the sky. Scripture says that he believed God and it was credited to him as righteousness (Genesis 15:5-6). From Abraham's perspective and from all earthly appearances, it was impossible for this promise to occur. Abraham was old; Sarah was old; they were both past the age of having children. But despite appearances and circumstances, Abraham believed God's promise which was revealed to him in a vision. In this way, Abraham became father to all of us, because we believe God's promise of eternal life in Jesus despite the appearance of tribulations and difficulties in this life. After the promise, Abraham still had to wait many years for Isaac to be born. Nevertheless, he kept believing, and when he was one hundred and Sarah was ninety, Isaac was born.

Or, consider when Joseph was a teenager and God gave him two dreams that indicated he would one day rule over his eleven brothers and even his parents. When he told his brothers of the dream, they got angry. Even his father, Jacob, indicated skepticism regarding Joseph's dream (Genesis 37:10-11). Then Joseph was sold into slavery by his brothers who thought that he would perish as a slave. They mocked Joseph's dreams, saying to one another what would happen to his big dreams (Genesis 37:18-20). As a slave, he was falsely accused and thrown into prison. It was not until Joseph was thirty that the fulfillment of the dreams came. That means that throughout Joseph's late teens and all of his twenties, his circumstances and all appearances indicated that his dreams had been wrong. How could an imprisoned slave ever reach a position of ruling? Yet, at age thirty, Joseph became ruler of the most powerful empire of his day, Egypt. In fact, not only was his dream fulfilled; it was fulfilled in a more magnificent manner than even the dreams indicated.

Let's look at David. As a boy, David, the youngest of his family, took care of sheep. When Samuel came to select Israel's future king, David's father didn't even bother to invite him to the dinner. But David was the one that God chose to replace Saul as king. In revealing his selection, God even warned Samuel not to judge by appearances. Sometime later, David—still a young man—killed the mighty warrior, Goliath, to the surprise of all present. Immediately, he was elevated to a general in Saul's army, he became Saul's son-in-law, and he became best friend to Jonathan, the apparent heir to the throne. Then, everything went sideways for David. Saul got jealous and tried to kill him. David had to flee for his life. He lived in the wilderness and eventually fled to Gath of all places, one of the Philistine cities. For his service to the king of Gath, he was given the town of Ziklag. From this town, he made raids into the countryside and attacked the enemies of God, but told the Philistines that he had attacked the towns of Judah. When the Philistines went to war against Israel, David wanted to join them, but they sent him back, because they thought he would betray them and fight for Saul. After he returned to Ziklag, he discovered that in his absence, the Amalekites had come, burned Ziklag, and captured all who were there. In their grief, David's men spoke of killing David. Scripture says that David strengthened himself in the Lord. From all appearances, David's situation was hopeless. Saul and all of Israel were against him, and even his own men had turned against him. But David strengthened himself in the Lord.

Have you ever wondered how in the world David did that? What does it mean to strengthen yourself in the Lord? Scripture doesn't tell us, but I believe David reminded himself of the prophecies and promises that had been given to him and spoken over him. If he was to be king of Israel, then his men couldn't kill him. His circumstances were lying to him. After strengthening himself, David gathered his men and set out after the Amalekites. They regained all they had lost. Shortly after returning to Ziklag, news came that Saul had been killed in battle. Within a short time, David ruled Judah from the city of Hebron and eventually all of Israel from Jerusalem. At the lowest point of his life, with his circumstances lying to him, David chose to believe the prophetic word spoken to him. From that point forward, everything began to change for David. Since the Philistines killed Saul and Jonathan in battle, the elders of Judah came to David requesting him to become their king. Samuel's previous announcement about David becoming king was coming true.

When Paul wrote to the Philippians, he was under house arrest after having been falsely accused in Jerusalem and imprisoned for two years in Caesarea because he wouldn't offer the Roman governor a bribe. After appealing to Caesar, he was transported to Rome, also after having endured a two-week storm and shipwreck upon Malta. For two years, he was under house arrest while awaiting his trial before Nero. In the midst of these circumstances, Paul exhorted the Philippians to rejoice and keep pursuing Jesus, because that was what was important.

While in seminary, I read books that spoke of discerning God's will for us. I was taught that one of the indicators of God's will for us is favorable circumstances that act as confirmation. However, what is odd about that teaching is it is difficult to find in the Bible. It wasn't true for Abraham, Joseph, David, Jesus, or Paul. So, what makes us so sure that our circumstances are an accurate predictor of God's will for us? Should we not remember his promises? This is the point. Our circumstances often lie to us and are a false indicator of our reality.

Many of us have promises and prophecies spoken to us that are, as of yet, unfulfilled. Furthermore, our circumstances scream at us, day in and day out, that those promises and prophecies cannot possibly be true. Circumstances said that Abraham would never be a father, but they were wrong. Circumstances affirmed that Joseph would never rule over anything, much less an empire, but he did. Circumstances declared that David would be killed in the wilderness, but he became king. Have you ever considered that your contrary circumstances may actually be an indicator of the truth of those promises and prophecies? Contrary circumstances may be all the more reason to rejoice and give glory to Father who, in the most amazing and dramatic fashion, will bring the promises to pass if we refuse to shrink back.

Let's pause now. Consider the promises, prophecies, and dreams that are in your life. Write them down or bring them to mind, for every child of God has a kingdom destiny. What is that destiny? Give thanks for that destiny. Now let's look at circumstances. If your circumstances are hindering you from pursuing your destiny, if they are hindering you from rejoicing, then it is time, like David, to strengthen yourself in the Lord. To focus on the promises which are heaven's reality and not be hindered in any way by temporary circumstances that seem to indicate the contrary. They may, in fact, be confirming the truth of those promises.

Questions for Reflection

1. Consider the source of your joy. Does it reflect the world's joy or kingdom joy?
2. In what ways might you increase kingdom joy in your life?
3. What are the prophecies that have been spoken to you for which you are still waiting?
4. What will be your response the next time you face discouraging circumstances?

SIX

How to Sustain Lasting Joy

WHAT DO THE BEATLES, Abraham Lincoln, Michael Jordan, Thomas Edison, Ulysses Grant, Lucille Ball, and Walt Disney have in common? Before becoming famously successful, they were more known for failure than success; nevertheless, they refused to give up. As followers of Jesus, we are called to something higher than individual fame and success. We are called to be like Jesus, and we will face adversity in reaching that call. However, it is one thing to hear about people who overcame adversity. It is another thing to know we will face adversity. But it is completely different to be in the midst of that adversity day in and day out and not give up.

In his letter, Paul told the Philippians to rejoice. Then he told them how to rejoice in the midst of adversity. If we can rejoice, even in the midst of adversity, then we will always know how to rejoice!

There is a big difference between knowing what we are to do, even studying what we are to do, and doing it—particularly when faced with adversity. Some time ago,

Donelle and I watched the movie, *42*. Since it is a sports movie, Donelle knew I would enjoy it. She was right. It's the story of Jackie Robinson, the first African American to play baseball in the major leagues since the 1880s. In 1946, Branch Rickey, the president of the Brooklyn Dodgers, recruited Robinson to play for the team. However, Rickey knew Robinson would face tremendous pressure and abuse. He made him agree that for three years, he could not fight back. Rickey knew his request was something that would be difficult for the strong and opinionated Robinson. Rickey warned Robinson of the abuse he would have to endure. In 1946, when Robinson played for the Montreal Royals, the Dodgers AAA farm club, and in 1947 when he played for the Brooklyn Dodgers, Robinson endured abuse from his teammates and fans in every city where he played. Some believe that the abuse he endured during those years shortened his life, because Robinson died at age 53 in 1972. Although Robinson knew he would face abuse and prepared for it, it was extremely difficult for him to live through it. While Rickey asked Robinson to endure the abuse, Jesus challenges his followers to also rejoice when faced with struggles. This is why I believe Paul gave additional teaching in Philippians 4 on the subject of rejoicing at all times.

Before speaking of joy, Paul reminded the Philippians of who they were. Their citizenship was in heaven, not on earth. They awaited Jesus' coming. Everything that has value on earth is heaven-related. The Philippians' citizenship and belonging was in heaven. Personal identity came through a name written in heaven. The Savior came from heaven. Treasure was to be invested in heaven, not risked on earth. The great transformation of life would be completed. Therefore, followers of Jesus were to stand firm and keep their eyes on Jesus (Hebrews 12:1-2). Focus on Jesus gives strength of conviction in spite of current circumstances.

Paul encouraged the Philippians to stand firm. Throughout his letters, he frequently urged his readers to stand firm in their faith relationship with Jesus. As the Corinthians faced many temptations to follow the world, Paul told them to stand firm in the faith (1 Corinthians 16:13). Perhaps more than any other city in the Roman world, Corinth embodied the materialistic and sensual lifestyle. The believers needed to know how to stand firm in such an adverse environment. To the Galatians being challenged to follow religious tradition, Paul urged them to stand firm in the liberty that Jesus acquired for them and not be deceived back into religious legalism (Galatians 5:1). The Galatians had a different challenge than the Corinthians. They faced Jewish false teachers who continually tried to persuade them that they had to follow Jewish tradition in order to follow Jesus.

We only tell someone to stand firm when we know they will face difficulty. For example, no mother ever tucks her children into bed for sleep and tells them to "stand firm." Rather, they tell them to "sleep well." Or, when you give your child a birthday party, you don't say "stand firm," because the party is to be enjoyable, not a difficulty to be endured. The command to "stand firm" is only appropriate because all Christians face adversity at one time or another. Jesus told his followers that in this world, they will face tribulation, but to take courage because he has overcome the world (John 16:33). In every case, the believer has to figure out how to stand firm in the face of the distractions the world offers. In our society, we are faced with many distractions, some moral and others immoral. For some of us, moral distractions—like family, work, and hobbies—pose greater danger to distract our hearts from Jesus than immoral distractions. For some Christians, the allure of becoming a Michael Jordan, Thomas Edison, or Lucille Ball may be more dangerous than abusing alcohol or drugs, as it may be an unnoticed distraction from becoming like Jesus.

In other words, we must remember our upward calling. It is to overcome all obstacles to become like Jesus, which is greater, higher, and different than overcoming all obstacles to become great in the world's opinion.

Paul's words to the Philippians to stand firm in the Lord refers to what we would call convictions. Paul urged the Philippians to stay true to their convictions regarding Jesus. Our convictions are what define our life and behavior. Joseph refused Potiphar's wife because of his conviction to honor God. Twice, David refused to take Saul's life because of his conviction to honor Saul, whom the Lord had anointed as king. Jesus chose to return to Jerusalem, knowing that the Jews planned to arrest and kill him, because of his conviction to honor his Father. The disciples refused to stop proclaiming that Jesus was alive, even though the Jews ordered them to stop. They were arrested and beaten because of their conviction to honor Jesus. Paul returned to Jerusalem, even though prophets warned him of hardship and abuse, because of his conviction to follow the Holy Spirit's leading. These examples reveal to us that our convictions lead us to do what we believe is right, no matter what the consequences are. As Jesus lived to follow and honor his Father, we live to follow and honor Jesus through being led by the Holy Spirit.

Furthermore, our convictions will define how we treat one another, so it should not surprise us that Paul urged two individuals in Philippi to live in agreement. Paul called them back to living a consistent life with who they are in Jesus. Living in harmony with one another is a natural result of standing firm in Jesus. On this occasion, he urged the two women to be of the same mind. Earlier, Paul urged all the Philippians to be like-minded (Philippians 2:2). While we don't know what the situation with these two women was (we are not even sure there was a conflict), from Paul's exhortations to be like minded throughout his letters, it is clear that being focused on the same thing is something to strive for. This is why the New Testament repeats over and over to keep the person of Jesus and the fellowship of the Holy Spirit clearly in mind. While we all may have different giftings, different concerns, and different assignments received from the Lord, our unity comes from our single-minded focus to honor Jesus.

We constantly face the Christian teaching that following Jesus is fulfilled by going to church, serving in that church, reading your Bible, praying, and living a moral life. While these things are important, knowing Jesus is much different than following a certain set of disciplines and traditions. We are to stand firm in the truth that we are to know Jesus and help others to know him. This conviction impacts the way we live our life every day, the decisions we make concerning speech, time and money management, and relationships. Jesus taught that his sheep hear his voice; therefore, knowing Jesus also includes learning to hear his voice, even in the midst of the challenges that face us every day. More challenging yet, we live life in an atmosphere that is soaked with a "get ahead and increase your income" mentality. It is hard to stand firm against that pressure and resist the temptation to keep up economically. We need to remember that our purpose here is not to succeed as the world defines success.

Perhaps the place we most clearly see the struggle to stand firm is in the lives of young people. I'm old enough to remember friends of mine who, in college, were highly dedicated to following Jesus. However, some got distracted with life: marriage, family, and career—all of which are good things. However, they no longer follow Jesus with the same passion they once did. They are good people, but it is clear from their life that Jesus is not their focal point. Their lives are filled with "good things," but the impact of Jesus lacks. The temptation to fit into middle class lifestyle, pursue career advancement, and pay a mortgage is very strong and potentially distracting from Jesus.

The command to stand firm with our attention focused on Jesus is foundational for sustaining joy in life. If we begin to live with a different purpose for our lives, then we will subtly begin to believe in an alternative source of joy.

I believe one of the great challenges for us as leaders is to find ways to teach people to stand firm in joyful Christian living—even though we spend the vast majority of our time in the world and its competing values. I know that in my life, I need much more time spent in Christian worship and community than is facilitated on Sunday morning and maybe an evening a week. The early church met for daily worship in the temple. This tradition continued in the church for centuries, as they held worship services each day. How do we encourage Christian worship and community throughout the work week in a way that is feasible for a modern schedule? The pursuit of an intimate relationship with Jesus must be a conviction for which we will sacrifice everything in order to sustain a joyful life. I have found that identifying ways I connect with Jesus and practicing those activities each day helps me be aware of Jesus' presence throughout my day.

This leads to addressing the question of why we should pursue sustaining joy. Paul gave a foundational reason for our joy—the nearness of Jesus with us. Jesus' nearness to us gives us no reason to be anxious, and actually, his nearness can give us great courage. When we know we are protected, we can do things we would never normally do. A couple years ago, a missionary speaker came to the church I was pastoring. His young son of three, who had recently broken his leg, was with him as he spoke. After holding his son for a while, the speaker put him down on the platform next to him as he shared about their ministry. I found myself watching the little boy. Normally, young children are uncomfortable being in front of so many people, but this little boy was quite at ease in front of the congregation. How could he be so comfortable when most would be anxious and comfortable? The little boy knew he was safe because his daddy was near to him, and he was confident that in his daddy's presence, nothing bad could happen to him.

The reality of Jesus' nearness means that we are safe. If

we are safe, we have absolutely no reason to be anxious. I recently heard a speaker explain that, according to studies, the most underdeveloped attribute in humans is gratitude. Because we have not developed gratitude in our lives, we fail to discern all that is good in our life. If we fail to focus on the good, then we give in to the tendency to focus attention on problems. Having focused on our problems, we are even less able to see the things for which we should be thankful.

Most of us fail to make a very important observation. All of us have some struggles in our life, but typically, we also have many more blessings than struggles. I remember a pastor saying that a multimillionaire told him that he would give everything he had if he could have a marriage like the pastor's. I wonder how many people wished they could have the multimillionaire's wealth and position, but failed to realize that the man lived with great pain and brokenness in his life, regardless. The man's comment was also a reminder to our pastor that he had been blessed by Jesus with a wonderful marriage. If we can focus on all that Jesus has done for us and give thanks, then the natural result in our life will be joy and peace. Joy, because of what we have been given, and peace, because we know that we are taken care of.

The way we think, day in and day out, gives to us a foundational key to sustaining joyful living on a daily basis. Joy is built upon the foundation of daily thinking in a manner that reflects our Father's heart. In order to remember what we've been given, we need to think in a correct manner.

Recently, I read an article written by a nurse who gave a practical explanation for doing what Paul wrote to the

Philippians. She explained that when we think, certain chemicals are released in our brain. Pleasant thoughts release dopamine, which causes us to feel good. In fact, the good feeling even outlasts our thoughts, because the chemical is still in our system after the thought has passed. On the other hand, when we dwell on negative thoughts, other chemicals are released that cause us to feel stressed and anxious. Again, even after we have corrected our thinking, we continue to feel stressed, because the chemicals are still in our system. That is why Paul instructed the Philippians to make sure that all their thoughts were focused on the positive truth rather than the negative lies.

Paul's instruction here should be self-evident. He tells us to dwell on what is true; why would we want to dwell on the false? He tells us to think about the honorable; why would we want to think about the dishonorable? Think about those things that are just; why would we fill our minds with injustice? Reflect on what is pure; why consider what is impure? Think about those things that are lovely; why consider something that is ugly? Think about something that is commendable, or worthy of praise; why would we think about that which is worthy of criticism?

While it seems obvious that we should think in this manner, it doesn't come naturally to us. I believe we can only think in this manner with the power of the Holy Spirit. While everyone knows we should think in this manner, those who typically have the power to do so are often those who have the Holy Spirit. I liken thinking in this manner to learning another language. When we went to Italy and began learning Italian, I assumed that language learning mainly consisted of learning a new vocabulary and grammatical system. Then, I clearly remember riding home on the bus after four hours in language school, and it hit me. It wasn't just learning words and grammar, but there were different ways of saying things. For example, in Italian, you don't say "Happy Birthday." You say "Good Completed Year." There was much more to learn than just words. I began to wonder if I would ever learn Italian, because it meant that I had to learn to think in a completely different manner, much like Paul told the Philippians to do. When I began language study, a colleague gave me invaluable advice. He said to avoid the temptation to translate from English when learning Italian. In other words, when you learn words, don't translate from English to Italian, but get a picture in your mind and then learn the Italian word for that picture. While it is initially easier and faster to translate from English to Italian, it later on slows you down in your speaking, because you've developed the habit of translating all your words. You also never really speak fluently, because many ways of saying something in English cannot be translated completely in Italian. For example, I spent months trying to say, "I've been waiting for ten minutes." Finally, one of my teachers, who also knew English grammar well, explained that in Italian, the English present perfect tense, "have (or has) been," doesn't exist. You have to express the concept in a completely different manner using only present tense. "I wait from ten minutes." I had to learn a completely new way of thinking.

I believe this is what Paul is telling us to do in Philippians 4; we are to think in a way that does not come naturally to us. Remember that Jesus told his disciples that what comes out of our mouth reveals what is in our heart. What Paul is doing is revealing to us a different thought language. It is a language that reveals the heart of God through the Spirit.

While most of us agree that we should think in this manner, I believe that there is subtle opposition to this way of thinking. I saw this when we were living in Rome. One day, I was speaking with our neighbor. I don't remember the topic of our conversation, but at one point, I commented about how our children enjoyed good health. Quite seriously, she told me not to speak in that manner. She believed talking about the positive aspects of our life brings a curse on us. It struck me how different that type of thinking is. If you live in a culture that discourages speaking about positive aspects of life, then you might be tempted to think negatively so that you don't somehow curse yourself.

I think we subtly have the same tendency in our culture. Recently, I was speaking with someone at work. I mentioned that we had not had any problem calls that day. He responded, "tongue in cheek," by saying, "let's not jinx it." Let's knock on wood so that it will continue. Now he was joking, but that line of thinking has a belief foundation from somewhere, otherwise it would not exist in our language. This type of speaking can discourage us from thinking in the manner Paul described, because we might fear "jinxing" the good things in our life. So, we subtly begin to think negatively and hope that positive things will occur. Not much different from how our Italian friend would think.

It is one thing to know that we are to think in a positive manner, but how do we actually do it? Many of us live in the midst of struggles and spend hours at work with people who do not share the kingdom values that we desire to have developed in our lives. We can apply the principles of language learning to help us learn to think joyfully and sustain joy. How do we learn another language? Many people spend years studying another language in school, but never learn to speak fluently. They can explain how the grammar works and translate the foreign words into English, but they cannot carry on a conversation. The reason is that you do not learn to speak a foreign language through study. Little children do not learn to speak by studying language, but by practicing what they hear others saying. Have you ever noticed that children of English speakers always learn English, never Spanish? But children of Spanish speakers always learn Spanish and not English. Kind of silly, but my point is that if you want to think in a godly manner, you have to spend time around those who do. Since most of us spend so much time around those who do not, then we must be very intentional about spending time around those who do. Living with lasting joy is not all that different from learning to speak another language.

Bible schools and seminaries try to teach us to think in godly ways through study, because you can measure what you study—but study is not always an effective means of producing godliness. However, some do learn to think biblically while at seminary or Bible college; why is that? I suggest to you that some learn to think biblically, because for several years, they lived in a community that thought that way, not so much because they studied it. This explains why many graduate from a biblically oriented college or seminary and think in godly manners, only to eventually stop doing so after graduating and returning to living in the world. They fail to maintain a community that helps them continue to think in a kingdom manner. While we can study those terms, we really learn to think that way by hanging out with, listening to, and speaking with those who already think in that manner. Transformation tends to be more a product of relationship than study. Study helps explain what happens, but transformation typically comes through relationship.

Our active, accomplishment-oriented culture wars against relational living and kingdom thinking. We are so busy that we have little time and energy for developing relationships and community. But somehow, we need to adjust the way we live so that we have the time and energy to develop kingdom thought patterns and help others do the same as we mature.

Worship music can also help us develop joyful thinking. Music tends to have a powerful emotional impact on us. I have found that I can be impacted more by listening to worship music than I can by listening to teaching. For much of my life, I thought listening to worship music was a waste of time; however, I've learned that it is often during those times of allowing worship music to impact me that I've gained greater understanding of Scripture.

I believe there is a connection between Paul's being able to be content in all circumstances and his instruction to the Philippians to think in a manner according to Philippians 4:8-9. I remember that for months, I had to think about every sentence I uttered in Italian. I had to think about every word, choose the correct form, and decide how they were to fit together. I remember our fourth level instructor giving us dictation, and I still struggled to keep up. He would read the words of a story, telling us where the punctuation was as he went. But because I was so focused on getting the words right, I would end up writing the words for "comma," "period," and "semi-colon," and then I would feel very foolish when it was corrected. My brain got so tired—but after a while, Italian became automatic. Thinking and even dreaming in Italian became normal. At times, even more comfortable than English. Certain concepts became easier to express in Italian than in English, and that was kind of weird. Similarly, it seems that Paul had become so adept at thinking in a kingdom pattern that the natural result was contentment. Having learned Italian and having learned to think in an Italian way gives me hope that someday I will be better at thinking in a kingdom way. However, it will require discipline to do so. As I would think about every word I spoke in Italian, I also need to think about every thought that comes into my mind. Paul told the Corinthians that we are to take every thought captive (2 Corinthians 10:5); that takes hard work and discipline, but it's not that different from learning a second language.

If we are immersed in kingdom thinking, then the natural result will be contentment in every circumstance. Contentment practiced in every circumstance becomes the foundation for us to express joy, even in times of difficulty.

Paul learned that, even in adversity, he could be content. We need to re-evaluate how we view adversity. For example, I love to run. However, since I was thirteen, I have also lifted weights, an activity that gives me no pleasure. The whole purpose of lifting weights is resistance, because you cannot build strength without resistance. I only do it because weight training helps me run. Let me suggest to you that exercise is to the physical body what adversity is to the spirit. We may not like it, but it is helpful in developing strength. Furthermore, without adversity, you will never develop greatness in the kingdom. If you consider anyone who was ever great in the kingdom or in the world, adversity was always part of their becoming great.

I grew up in Wisconsin during the 1960s. Virtually everyone I knew was a Packer fan. On December 31, 1967, the Packers played the Dallas Cowboys for the NFL Championship in Green Bay. The temperature was thirteen below, and the field became ice as the game progressed. Some players had to be treated for frostbite after the game. Some have called that game the greatest football championship ever played. With a little more than four minutes left in the game, the Packers, who were behind, got the ball. They had to score a touchdown to win the game, but they had not done well since the second quarter. With thirteen seconds left in the game, the ball sat on the one-yard line, and the Packers called their last time out and decided on play. The play was a quarterback sneak that Bart Starr ran, and he went on to score the winning touchdown. Many people have heard of that game, often called the Ice Bowl. I suggest to you that what made that game great was the adverse conditions under which it was played. If it had not been played in the cold and ice, it probably would not be remembered that much, because many games and even championships end with a last second score.

However, what many people don't know is that seven years prior, the Packers were in a similar situation. In 1960, they were playing for the championship in Philadelphia. They got the ball one final time with just a few minutes left, needing to score a touchdown to win. They got down near the Philadelphia goal line, but they were stopped short and lost the game. After the game, Green Bay coach, Vince Lombardi, told his team that they would never be in that situation again. In fact, over the next seven years, the Packers never lost a play-off or championship game. I suggest to you that the victory in the midst of adverse conditions during the Ice Bowl had its foundation in the adversity and pain of losing the championship in 1960.

Many of us face adversity today, but we have reason for hope and joy. As we stand firm in joy by rejoicing, we know that Jesus is near. We can give thanks for what is good in our life, and we can discipline ourselves to think according to Father's heart until it becomes automatic in our life.

Questions for Reflection

1. In what areas do you face adversity?
2. How might your present adversity be the foundation for a victory to come?
3. How might you change your thinking so that you see adversity as a reason for joy?

SEVEN

The Veil Has Been Removed

WHEN I WAS in my first month of language learning, I heard many words I didn't understand, but occasionally I heard a specific word that sounded familiar, and I was tempted to assume I knew what it meant. That word was "piú," pronounced "pew" in English (like something stinky, rather than seats in church). I remember being amused. Eventually, I discovered that "piú" in Italian means "more," not "stinky." I had encountered what, in language learning, is called a false friend. It is a word that I may think I understand, but I have associated a wrong meaning to it.

I suggest that, as we learn to live out the kingdom of Jesus on earth, we sometimes encounter a similar phenomenon. Things happen to us, and we associate earth's meaning to it, without realizing that heaven has a different meaning and purpose for that same event.

As we encounter Father, we discover that he is very different than we are. Because he is so different, we may respond to him in fear. We see this over and over in Scripture. Let's start with Moses and the people of Israel. While Moses hungered for the glory of God, the people feared it.

Moses asked God to show him his ways. He told God if his presence would not be with him, he did not want to leave that place. Moses wanted to stay where God was. Either God came with him, or he would stay (Exodus 33:12-15). God assured Moses that he would go with them. However, that was not enough for Moses; he wanted to see God's glory. God told Moses that Moses could see all his goodness, but his face he could not see and live (16-20). Therefore, God would shield Moses from his face, but Moses could see the glory of God's goodness after God had passed by (20-23).

The next morning, God told Moses to ascend the mountain with two new tablets; these were to replace the two that had been broken in the Golden Calf episode. After the event of the Golden Calf, God invited Moses back up the mountain (Exodus 34:1-2). Moses was to come alone, and not even the flocks were to graze on the mountain. When Moses reached the top of the mountain, the Lord revealed his glory to Moses, provoking Moses' worship. Moses remained on the mountain forty days and forty nights with no water or food, and when he came down, his face glowed (34:27-30). When the people saw Moses' face, they were afraid. Because of their fear, Moses covered his face with a veil, which he removed only to speak with the Lord in the tent of meeting (34:33-35).

Is it not a curious contrast between Moses and the people? Moses hungered for the glory of God, and it physically changed him. However, the people were afraid, not only of the glory and power of God, but of its reflection on Moses' face.

The concept of a veil became a theme throughout the history of Israel. Throughout God's interactions with the people of Israel, he always veiled his presence. When Moses constructed the Tabernacle, he put a veil (curtain) to separate the Holy of Holies where the ark was (Exodus 40:3). Since the ark was the representation of God's presence, it was veiled from the people. Solomon did the same thing when he built the temple (2 Chronicles 5:7-9). From the time of Moses until the death of Jesus, the presence of God was veiled from the people. However, when Jesus died on the cross, an amazing event took place. The veil was split down the middle from top to bottom, revealing the presence and glory of Father that had always been veiled from the people (Matthew 27:50-51). The veil was first indicated by the hand of God covering Moses, then the veil over Moses' face, the veil in the Tabernacle, and finally the veil in the temple. After the splitting of the veil in the temple, there is now nothing preventing us from seeing the face of Father. Since we are in Christ and seated in the heavenlies like Jesus, we can see the face and glory of God. In other words, since there is no veil between Jesus and Father, then no veil exists between us and the glory of Father.

Yet, for many people, a self-created veil remains. Consider what Paul wrote concerning the veil of the law. Paul referred to Moses veiling his face from the Israelites. He pointed out that, even after the coming of Jesus, people's hearts were veiled from the truth (2 Corinthians 3:12-15). Rather than embracing the glory of God, which is now open to all, people still live like the Jews did under the law. They prefer to follow religious rules instead of entering into a divine, glory-revealing relationship with

Jesus. Those whose hearts are still veiled by religious law struggle to understand what Augustine meant when he said to love God and do as you please. If you are committed to following religious rules, then you cannot do as you please, because what you please will lead you to sin. However, if the Spirit of Jesus has taken up residence with your spirit, then you are free. Love, not rules, governs behavior. "What you please" becomes good, not sin, because a lover always lives to please the beloved. When the veil of religious rules is removed, a person becomes free to love and no longer needs rules to govern his behavior. However, many religious people fear such an approach, because they are convinced it will lead to undisciplined living and sin. Their fear reveals all the more how committed they are to rules and how their hearts are veiled from the freeing presence of Father.

Fear of love's freedom hinders us from God's glory and results in misunderstanding the ways of God. We misunderstand his language, just like I misunderstood the meaning of the Italian word "piú." We misunderstand the ways that he reveals himself and his glory to us. Throughout Scripture, we see God revealing himself. Yet, many misunderstand his presence.

Have you ever noticed that, in Scripture, Father often reveals himself in times of tribulation and removes his presence from people he has blessed greatly? I know that sounds strange, but let me give you some illustrations. Why would his presence be in something that he doesn't send (tribulation) and his absence be in something that he does (blessing)? I suggest to you that it may involve the meaning of each—meanings that we may often misunderstand.

In John 16:33, Jesus said, "in the world there is tribulation. But take heart; I have overcome the world." Jesus linked tribulation with courage, or to "take heart." Tribulation should not discourage us, because Jesus has already overcome the world. What does that mean? Jesus has already defeated every tribulation that is found in the world. The word, "tribulation," literally means "pressure." Tribulation is a defeated foe. We may experience tribulation or the world's pressure, but it is already defeated by Jesus. Its power to do us harm has been removed. While we may feel the pressure, it cannot hurt us. When I had my wisdom teeth removed, the oral surgeon gave me sodium pentothal. I was so relaxed that I felt no pain; I only felt pressure in my mouth and heard drilling. In other words, I felt pressure, but the pain was removed.

In Romans 8:29-39, Paul explained that, because of what Jesus has done and who we are in him, nothing in this world can harm us. Even though we live in a world filled with evil, evil cannot harm us. This is something that is hard to believe in a world that is filled with accidents, sickness, and death. Often, the problem with tribulation is that we feel fear when it comes our way, just as the world does. The world has no hope, so if something bad happens, the person of the world has no refuge and no protection. They have no choice but to assume the worst-case scenario. Sometimes followers of Jesus believe the lie that, because of the tribulation they experience, Father has abandoned them or that they have done something to cause Father to teach them a lesson—but tribulation is not punishment from Father. That is ascribing to tribulation the world's meaning, not heaven's.

As followers of Jesus living under his protection, we

have no reason to assume a worst-case scenario. Rather, we can approach tribulation from a completely different perspective. If what Paul said in Romans 8 is true, then we know the following. If I am a child of God, then everything that happens to me will result in good, even if its origin is completely evil. Whatever it is, it cannot separate me from Jesus' presence in my life. Therefore, rather than assuming the worst, I can look at the tribulation and ask, "what is heaven's goal in my experiencing this?" What good is Father producing through this tribulation? In other words, a kingdom perspective can transform a tribulation into an encounter with Father. For the child of God, tribulation doesn't mean "stink" (pew); it means "more" of Father's presence (piú).

As I look back over my life, I see that this has taken place. I have not responded to all tribulation in my life with heaven's meaning. Actually, I have responded this way to very few tribulations, but there is one dramatic one I remember. When our daughter, Sara, was almost two years old, Donelle was expecting another baby. One morning, about four months into the pregnancy, she began to hemorrhage. We called the doctor—she told us to get Donelle into the hospital, and she would meet us there. However, Donelle had already lost too much blood and could not stand without passing out. I called the doctor again, and she sent an ambulance. At that time, in Italy, you could not call 911 for an ambulance; only a doctor could summon one. When this took place, my parents were visiting us. We had planned to leave for Switzerland the following day. I accompanied Donelle in the ambulance to the hospital. The paramedics didn't realize how well I understood Italian, so I could tell by their conversation that the situation was serious. They wasted no time getting Donelle to the hospital, racing through the crowded streets of Rome. When we arrived, they whisked her away, leaving me alone in a hallway. I found a plastic chair and sat down. The thought occurred to me that I may have seen Donelle alive for the last time. As I sat in that plastic chair in the hallway, a peace that I have never known enveloped my entire being. I didn't know what form my future would take, but I knew everything would be all right. Eventually, the doctor emerged and told me Donelle would be all right. While sitting and waiting to find out the news, I should have been anxious and concerned, which, by the way, is my normal reaction to tribulation. But, abnormally for me, I felt such a powerful peace that I had never felt before or after. That feeling was not from me; it was from heaven. With love and grace, the Spirit invaded my being and filled me with something I could not conjure up myself. I didn't consciously think about the situation from heaven's perspective, but Jesus just showered his grace upon me. My tribulation that morning became an encounter with heaven that I will never forget.

When we view tribulation from heaven's perspective, we can also help others to do the same. Consider Joseph who, after spending more than a decade in slavery and prison, became the governor of Egypt. Through Joseph, his entire family found food and shelter in the richest part of Egypt. After a period of time, Jacob, Joseph's father, died. His ten brothers, who had sold him into slavery, became fearful for what they expected Joseph to do. Actually, they assumed that Joseph was like them, so they feared that Joseph would do what they would do if they were in his position. They went to Joseph and told him that their father wanted Joseph to forgive them. But Joseph wasn't like them at all. When he heard what they said, he wept. While Joseph knew that his brothers had meant to do him evil, he had understood that God meant it for good (Genesis 50:19-21). Joseph used the position that God had placed him in to do good to the same brothers who had intended evil against him. Joseph had learned to view his tribulation from heaven's perspective. He refused to focus on what he had lost and suffered, but rather, he saw God's good intentions to bless and protect his people. Two thousand years before Jesus, Joseph encountered the Spirit of God and received freedom. Joseph, the one who had been a slave and prisoner, was free, while his brothers who had never been enslaved or imprisoned, were stuck in chains.

All of us face tribulation, so how do we respond to it? When tribulation comes into our life, we have an opportunity to encounter God, but we tend to give it a meaning of bad and evil. We need to learn a new language with new words and new meanings. All tribulation that touches our life starts out evil, then it is filtered through the protective presence of Holy Spirit and becomes a place of encounter with Holy Spirit. Although it often does, tribulation should not cause fear in our life, because it is a place in which we can experience Father's love in ways previously not experienced. We need to remember that Scripture says God is near the broken-hearted (Psalm 34:18). When you and I experience tribulation, which is the result of living in a fallen world, and not sent by God, he is closer to us than when we feel blessed and comfortable.

When I was seven years old, I contracted pneumonia and ended up in the hospital. In those years, my grandparents spent their winters in California with my uncles and their families. However, when my grandfather heard that I was sick, he told my grandmother they were leaving early. He drove straight through, pulling an Airstream trailer at eighty miles an hour down the highway to get back to my bedside. Now, my grandfather loved me before I got sick, but when I got sick, he dropped everything to be near me. This is exactly like our Father. When we face tribulation, it is as if heaven stops so that Father can be near to us. We must remember these truths so that we can have the strength to enjoy his glory when we do experience tribulation.

While we often misinterpret tribulation, I believe we do the same with blessing. Blessing comes to us starting out as good, because it comes from Father. But, throughout Scripture, people who were blessed often fell. It happened over and over, until in Luke 18, Jesus declared how hard it was for a rich man to enter into the kingdom of heaven. The disciples couldn't believe their ears when Jesus said that. Think about it. The people who have received God's blessing have the hardest time entering into the kingdom! King Saul was blessed when he was anointed king over Israel. It was God who made him king. Nevertheless, in the midst of all that blessing, he fell to the extent that God had to remove him. David fell into sin with Bathsheba, not when he was in tribulation, but when he was at the height of his power—rich and secure in his palace. Solomon, the wisest and richest man who didn't have an enemy in the world, fell into idolatry at the end of his life. In the decades prior to

Assyria's invasion, Israel experienced great wealth and blessing. Prior to Babylon's invasion, Judah experienced blessing and even revival under King Josiah.

We have to be missing something here, because God is the one who blesses us for good purposes. So, why do blessings often end up badly? It can't be Father's fault, so we must be missing something. That something, I believe, is our worldly meaning given to the blessing. I believe the reason blessing is given is the same as heaven's purpose in tribulation. Father desires an encounter with us. In tribulation, Father encounters us and produces strength. In the blessing, Father offers partnership to produce intimacy. The problem is that we often don't give that meaning to the blessing.

We see this most plainly in the parable of the talents. The master blessed three men. To the first man, the master (Father) gave five talents. The man, without fear of losing the talents, produced five more for a total of ten. With joy, the man showed his master the ten talents. The master invited him into a joyful relationship with him. The second received two talents and responded in the same way as the first. Without fear of loss, he used the two and gained two more. He too, with joy, presented them to the master and received the same reward. However, the third man took his talent and became fearful of losing it. He had been blessed with a talent, but he lived in fear of losing it. So, he spent his time protecting his blessing rather than using it. When the master returned, the man gave him the talent and explained his fear. This man was rejected. The third man was blessed, but his fear of losing the blessing condemned him (Matthew 25:14-30). Two responded in partnership and cast fear away. They used the talents for the kingdom. The third man responded in fear. Just as tribulation can cause fear in our life, so can blessing. The third man responded like King Saul did to his being king. Rather than using his position to bless Israel and partner with God, he lived to protect his position. He eventually lost the blessing and his life.

When Father blesses us, we must not respond in fear of losing it. Yet, this becomes harder the older we become, because Father gives us more and more. When I was in college, I didn't have much materially. I had a great heritage from my family, but I owned little more than a car, a stereo, clothes, and some textbooks. If I lost all my worldly possessions, it would not have been a great loss. However, as time went by, Father gave me a wife, children, and way more stuff than any of us need. With each new blessing comes an increased temptation to protect what I have. Fear and anxiety bangs at the door of my heart to enter in with all kinds of "what if" scenarios. With nothing, it is easy to live like the first two men in the parable of the talents, but with each increasing blessing, the temptation to slip into a life like the third man becomes increasingly attractive.

In each season of life, God invites us into a partnership of managing and stewarding the blessings. The blessings are to produce an encounter with God and bring blessing to others, but we often don't use them in that way. We tend to sink into fear of losing them, believing the lie that Father may want to take them away from us. Like tribulation, we must grasp heaven's meaning for blessings, not earth's. God gives blessings for heaven's purposes, not only our personal comfort and enjoyment.

As we manage them in partnership with Father, we enter into Father's joy. Once we receive a blessing, we have a choice. We can partner with the Spirit and multiply the blessing into a kingdom advance. Or we can hoard it and hide it because we are afraid to lose it. The third man lost his talent; King Saul lost his kingdom. David and Solomon lost their peaceful reigns.

We see this principle at work in Abraham and Isaac. Isaac was the God-given son of promise. He was the blessed miracle son; yet at one point, God asked Abraham to sacrifice his son. In that moment, Abraham had to deal with fear. The fear of losing the blessing, his beloved son. But he refused to give into fear. He would rather partner with God than protect Isaac. God was pleased with Abraham's choice, and Abraham's relationship with God reached a new level of intimacy. Even the blessing of Isaac could not come between Abraham and God. Abraham's decision to reject fear of the blessing's loss is forever recorded as a remarkable act of faith in Hebrews 11.

The whole purpose of our life is to expand heaven's kingdom on earth. We are not called to do this alone and without Father's resources. In Philippians 4, Paul reminded the Philippians that the Lord (Jesus) is near to us. That means we are never alone. Just because we cannot physically see Jesus doesn't mean that he is not near. I could not see the peace that enveloped me in that Roman hospital in the summer of 1995, but I assure you that it was more real than anything I have ever experienced. I could not see Jesus or Father next to me, but they were there, because Scripture says that Father draws near to the broken-hearted. We can see that David understood this through Psalm 34. Listen to his words. "When the righteous cry for help, the Lord hears and delivers them out of all their troubles" (v. 17). The righteous, that is those who are in Jesus, cry for help. That means we will need help, but Jesus will deliver us out of our troubles. The Lord is near the brokenhearted and saves the crushed in spirit. When I experienced Jesus' peace, I didn't understand it. I didn't understand why we lost that baby. And then—almost a year and half later—Brian was born healthy in that very same hospital, delivered by the same doctor who had come and told me Donelle would be alright. All I know is that Jesus was with me; he filled me with peace, and he removed, over time, the pain of loss. I can't explain it; he just did it.

James understood the principle as well, as he explains that we can also cause Father to draw even closer to us. James tells us to draw near to God, and he will draw near to us. How do we do that? We embrace humility; we submit ourselves to Father, we resist Satan and his lies, we cleanse our actions, and we purify our heart. We refuse to speak against our brothers (James 4:7-12).

I believe Father wants to take us on a grand adventure that we call life. Our life is not meant for us to seek out the easiest and most comfortable path, but it is meant for us to encounter Father in every situation we face. He will encounter us when we turn to him in our adversity. He will encounter us when we seek him out in our blessing.

I believe that as we learn to speak the language of heaven regarding our tribulations and blessings, then we, like Paul, can affirm that we have learned to be content in whatever situation in which we find ourselves—because in that situation, we will find that Jesus is with us. We live in a society that is dying to find life; they are turning to all kinds of false gods, but we have the answer to what their hearts seek. We, more than all others, need to learn to live speaking heaven's language so others will learn it as well. Let me ask you, what can be better than that?

Questions for Reflection

1. So, take a moment. What situation do you find yourself in today?
2. Are you in tribulation? Take a moment and ask the Holy Spirit how he wants to meet you within that tribulation, in ways that can only take place through this time of suffering.
3. Are you being blessed? Don't let fear of losing what you have dictate your actions; ask the Spirit how he wants to partner with you as you manage that blessing to multiply its kingdom impact.

EIGHT

Being Transformed Through Relationship

IN COLLEGE, one of my mentors told me that when you are young, you are idealistic and that, at some point, you need to leave idealism behind and accept realism. At the time, around 20 years old, I believed him. Eventually, I became a realist; I stopped dreaming about seeing the impossible come about and started living in the possible. Spiritually, that concept dried me up completely. You see, this well-intentioned advice wars against what Jesus taught. Kingdom living is rejecting the belief that we are limited by what humans call possible and, rather, seeking what merely masquerades as impossible. The problem for many Christians is that they have settled for what is possible at the expense of the impossible, which Father wants to accomplish through us.

It occurred to me that you can describe the history of Christianity with one word, "distraction." The early church got distracted by the Jewish Law, which Paul had to address with the Galatians. The Roman and Byzantine churches got distracted with promoting imperial Rome so much that they preserved imperial culture more than a kingdom one. In the Middle Ages, the church got distracted by conquering the wealth of the Holy Land. In the Reformation, doctrine and Scripture became the focus, both of which have become a distraction even to this day. Today, Christians seem more concerned about someone's doctrine than whether that individual knows and loves Jesus. Even when good things distract us, they are dangerous because they distract us from Jesus. Today, much of the church is distracted by the things of God—doctrine and social issues, for example—but often miss Jesus in the process.

Several years ago, as Jesus was saving me from the deadness of "realism," I had lunch with two friends. Our conversation challenged what I had previously thought. One of the men told me his story. He had been a pastor and powerfully worked in the supernatural, but he said he had done so without intimacy. His confession shocked me. I understood how you can have theological and biblical knowledge but not have intimacy with God—but I had assumed that everyone who walked in supernatural power must have intimacy with God. Nevertheless, here was my friend telling me the very opposite. He said that eventually he lost all that he had previously valued and was alone one day, grieving over his losses. The Holy Spirit came to him and asked if intimacy with God was not enough for him. He realized in that moment that intimacy with God is worth everything in the world. I suggest to you that intimacy with Father is the foundation of the transformed life.

Transformation was one of the practical themes that Paul taught the Romans in his great letter to them

(Romans 11:30-12:3). Beginning in chapter 9, Paul explained what happened to Israel. They rejected Jesus, but their rejection of Jesus led to the entry into the kingdom of all nations (Gentiles). Paul argued in chapter 11 that there would come a time when Israel would believe, bringing great blessing to all. So, when we get to the end of 11 and the beginning of 12, this is the context.

Over and over in Scripture, we read that Father loves humankind and desires a relationship with everyone. Anyone who loves understands the fundamental nature of mercy to maintain and develop any relationship. Not to exercise mercy means the end of a relationship. All of us were at one time disobedient to Father. We were cut off from him. To the Ephesians, Paul explained Father's mercy toward us (Ephesians 2:1-7). For who of us can say that we had no need of Father's mercy toward us? Paul went on to say that one day God will display this same type of extraordinary mercy toward the Jewish people to bring them into relationship with Jesus. Believers who love Jesus will be instrumental in bringing Jewish people into this relationship.

Paul explained that Father's mercy is beyond our capacity to understand (Romans 11:33-36). He described God's ways as both unsearchable and unfathomable. These two words can be taken in two ways. They can refer either to something that has not yet been searched out or understood. The other sense is to understand these two words to refer to something that is impossible to understand with human means. Peter used the form of "unsearchable" to describe how the prophets sought out the salvation which we now enjoy. The salvation which we now enjoy is what the angels longed to look upon (1 Peter

1:10-12). Paul used the word "unfathomable" again in his letter to the Ephesians to describe his mission (Ephesians 3:8-20). He made an extraordinary statement to the Ephesians which reminds us of our purpose. He declared to the Ephesians that it was his responsibility to communicate that which was "unfathomable." In other words, God had given to him a responsibility that without divine understanding and power was impossible to accomplish. Jesus had given to Paul what today we would call "Mission Impossible." Without divine understanding and ability, you cannot communicate that which is unfathomable. This is what Paul goes on to say. Father does more than what we ask or think (Ephesians 3:20-21). We need to understand that Father is doing much more than what he appears to be doing in our life.

Paul quoted two fascinating passages. In Romans 11:34, he quoted Isaiah 40:13; Isaiah 40 describes a life that is impossible to live without divine power and the unfathomable ways of God (Isaiah 40:21-31). As God never tires, he gives strength to the weary. The exhausted will run and not tire. How's that for a paradox? I love to run, but I become tired. In the natural realm, physical exertion causes fatigue, but in the kingdom, Father supplies power—even when you are weak and weary—so that you are stronger than when you were energetic and rejuvenated. This passage describes a kingdom life that lives continually dependent upon God. This makes absolutely no sense in the natural, but it makes perfect sense in the kingdom.

In Romans 11:35, Paul quoted a seemingly odd book to explain God's unfathomable mercy. He quoted two passages in Job, a book not commonly associated with mercy, but more with suffering. First, Paul quoted Job 35:7 which is from Elihu's rebuke of Job. Elihu was the young man who responded to Job just prior to God addressing Job. In fact, Elihu's discourse foreshadows much of what God was about to say, which may be the reason why he was not rebuked by God as Job's friends were. Second, Paul quoted what God said to Job in Job 41:11. Each of these quotes underscore the fact that we do not naturally know God's way, nor can we in any way place God in our debt. These quotes from Job caused me to ponder why the Spirit would lead Paul to quote this book. It occurred to me that many of us have missed the point of Job. We tend to think of Job as a book of suffering and loss, because Job lost his wealth, his kids, and his health. Questions arise like "how could God let this happen, and why do bad things happen to good people?"

It occurred to me that we may have placed emphasis in the wrong place regarding Job. Rather than being a book about suffering, it is actually a book about revelation and transformation, exactly what Paul is talking about in Romans 11. Although Job was a righteous man, he didn't know God very well. Rather than living in joy for what he had received, he lived in fear of losing what he had. He offered sacrifices out of the fear that his children may have committed some sin (Job 1:5). After losing his wealth, children, and health, he declared that what he had feared happened (Job 3:25). Job feared losing the good life he enjoyed; then he lost it. These are words of a religious and distracted man. Rather than enjoying what God had blessed him with, he lived in fear of losing what he had received. Job reflects the danger that anyone with wealth faces. Although Job was righteous and declared blameless, he needed to be transformed. This is exactly what God did for him. At the end of the book, Job encounters God and is transformed so that he could declare that before, he had only heard of God. Before, Job had worshiped God from afar, but then he said his eyes saw God. That acknowledgment of God caused Job to repent (Job 42:1-6). Remember that Job's transformation came while his suffering continued. Neither his health nor his wealth were restored until after Job had prayed for (and forgiven) his friends (Job 42:10). I suggest that the message of Job is not so much about suffering, as it is about the truth that an encounter with God is worth everything. Job is more about Father's mercy that led to his revealing himself to Job, rather than the pain that Job endured after losing his children, wealth, and health.

When Paul began Romans 12, he began with the word "therefore." The transformation of which he speaks in chapter 12 is based on what he had already taught in chapter 11. Our transformation is founded upon encountering Father through his mercy, shown to us in Jesus. Our lives are a response to encountering Father through Jesus, because the best part of being a follower of Jesus is not forgiveness; it's not provision; it's not supernatural power, but it is Jesus. Solomon shows us in the book of Ecclesiastes that to have everything and not have a relationship with God is meaningless.

Nevertheless, Paul indicated in Romans 12:2 that there was a battle. If there weren't, he would not have reminded the Romans to avoid being conformed to this world. Even though God demonstrates supernatural mercy and bestows blessings, there remains a temptation and consequently a battle against being conformed to this world. There are times when we must confront and battle the lies that face us. To give into the despair of those lies will result in being conformed to this world.

What are some of those lies? I have noticed that many lies are tied to our past, or what the world says about who we are. Some believe that, because they never got a college education, they are now stuck; that their opportunities are behind them. In the world, that may be true, but for those of us who know and follow Jesus, we have resources and opportunities available through our relationship with Father; we have reason for hope. Others believe that since they are of a certain age, they can no longer make significant contributions. Others may believe they are limited because of their gender or ethnic background. To be conformed by the world is to be placed in a box mainly composed of lies that we've been told by people who have not come to know the liberating power of Jesus.

To be transformed, then, is to believe all of what Jesus taught us. We are not limited by ethnicity, race, gender, social standing, age, ability, education, finances, etc., but only by how close we live out our Father's heart and the mind of Jesus. If Jesus told the disciples to feed the five thousand even though they only had a few loaves of bread and a couple of fish, then what does that mean to us? If Jesus commanded the disciples to go cast out demons, heal the sick, and raise the dead in his name, then what does that mean for us? If Jesus said that any one of us who believes in Jesus would do greater works than he himself did, then what does that mean for us? If Jesus said that the least of us who follow him would be greater than even John the Baptist, then what does that mean for us?

What I find I need to do in my life is to not look at circumstances as either positive or negative; to not give room to the lies that are prevalent in our world; but to keep my mind, heart, and soul firmly fixed on what Jesus says and promises.

Questions for Reflection

1. How might the difficulties that you face in your life actually reflect Father's desire to reveal himself to you?
2. What lies have you believed that tend to conform you to the world?
3. What "impossible" things do you believe Father is leading you to accomplish with his power?

NINE

Living Out a Transformed Life

ONE OF THE struggles of living a transformed life is dealing with our failures. Just as we experience failures, so also did the disciples, illustrated in the story found in Matthew 17:14-23. It is the story of Jesus healing the demonized boy after nine of the disciples were unable to.

Before we consider the story, I want to make a couple observations about what happened before Jesus arrived on the scene. Immediately before arriving, Jesus, Peter, James, and John had been on the mountain, where Jesus had been transfigured before the disciples' eyes. While transfigured, Jesus met with two of the great Old Testament prophets, Moses and Elijah. Immediately, the three disciples were thunderstruck by Father's voice from a cloud, declaring Jesus to be his beloved son and to listen to him. As they came down the mountain, Jesus warned them not to speak of this event until after he had risen from the dead, but they did not understand what rising from the dead meant. Then they asked Jesus about Elijah, who was to come before the Messiah. Jesus explained that Elijah had come but had not been recognized. The disciples, according to Matthew, grasped that Jesus was referring to John the Baptist. It was at this point that they happened upon the crowd who was surrounding the other nine disciples as teachers of the law were arguing/debating with the disciples.

If you are like me, a question arises from reading this passage. What were they arguing/debating about? Mark pointed out that the scribes were arguing with the nine disciples. The word "argue" can also mean "debate." It is likely that the scribes questioned the disciples' ability/authority to cast out demons, because the boy's father explained that he had brought his son to them and that they were unable to heal him—a key theme throughout this passage. The boy's father pointed out their inability. The disciples also asked Jesus about their inability. The disciples' struggle is often the one that we face as we desire to live a supernaturally transformed life. This is the difference that we often see between what should be—as seen in Scripture—and what we see lived out. Jesus had given the disciples authority to heal and to cast out demons (Mark 6:7-12). Then they went out and did so. It must have been difficult for them to encounter a situation where they were unable to free the boy.

Similar to the disciples of the 1st century, Christians of the 21st century will encounter those who are skeptical about the supernatural. The scribes challenged Jesus' authority, and the disciples' failure to heal the boy probably fueled the scribes to step up their attacks on Jesus as well as the disciples' authority in the spiritual realm. Many Christians deny the power of the supernatural today, because there is an alarming lack of its exercise.

What is interesting about the denial of supernatural power today is that it is based on the same argument that was used against Jesus. The disciples' failure caused the scribes and even the boy's father to doubt whether Jesus had the power and authority to heal the man's son.

Many teach that the supernatural was limited to the time of Jesus and the apostles. This stance suggests that God may heal today through prayer, but he doesn't empower anyone with the gift of healing. The explanation usually goes something like: If you read through the book of Acts, it seems like the supernatural diminishes. I remember hearing that explanation and realizing it did not hold up under examination. For example, in the latter chapters of Acts, we read that the daughters of Philip were prophets, which means that the supernatural was not limited to the generation of the apostles, because Philips daughters were not apostles. They belonged to the second generation of Christians, nevertheless they lived out supernatural power. Paul operated with supernatural power in the latter chapters of Acts when he healed many on the island of Malta. The Church Fathers prior to the Council of Nicaea also wrote of supernatural power present among Christians.

The problem is that generations of Christians have been taught that the gifts of healing have disappeared. Strangely, these same Christians affirm the idea that Scripture is the only foundation for faith and practice; yet, they teach a doctrine that cannot be found in Scripture. Think about it. What is the average Christian going to do, disagree with well-known Bible teachers who write books and speak on the radio, teaching that healing and the supernatural is not from God because it disappeared?

Many choose to keep following what they were taught and not cross-check that teaching with Scripture. Nevertheless, we are to live like the disciples. They chose to follow Jesus, and this brought them into conflict with all the well-known Bible teachers of the day. In this case, the disciples didn't have victory over the demonic, but the skeptical scribes were not correct either. Since living in supernatural transformation is not normal, there will often be knowledgeable skeptics. However, we are still called to pursue and live out the supernatural, unfathomable life that Jesus offers to us.

It was Jesus who gave the explanation for the disciples' inability. Jesus indicated one of the problems in Matthew 17:19 and raised the next question. Why did Jesus call them an unbelieving generation? We can understand why Jesus would have referred to the scribes as unbelieving, because they refused to place their faith in Jesus. We can understand why Jesus would have said this to the boy's father, because he confessed his own unbelief (Mark 9:24). But the real difficulty was with the disciples. In Matthew 17:20, Jesus told them that their problem, first and foremost, was the "littleness of their faith." Actually, he used the word for unbelief. It was their unbelief that hindered them. So, the big question is, how did the disciples display unbelief? Before we look at that question, we need to define unbelief.

Sometimes, we may think we understand a word when, really, we don't. In English, there is a difference between the words "belief" and "faith." The word "belief" tends to have more of an intellectual connotation in the sense of verbally affirming or proclaiming something. We have doctrinal statements which we verbally affirm. Faith, on the other hand, is more a matter of the heart and can often be described as trust. In modern society, you can say you believe something in your mind, but that doesn't not necessarily mean you trust. You can affirm something, even when that truth doesn't transform your life. In the New Testament, that form of "belief" is not "belief." Rather, the word translated "believe" or "belief" is the same as the word, "faith." That means if you have no trust, you have no belief. Trust is displayed by the appropriate *action* which reflects trust or belief. I can say that I believe a chair will support my weight, but I have no faith until I sit in it and depend on it to hold me up.

What most people don't realize is that everyone has faith and exercises faith. The bigger question is what they have faith in. By depositing our money in the bank, we exercise faith that the bank will keep it safe. By sitting down and enjoying a meal, we exercise faith in the person who prepared it and the store where it was purchased. By drinking water from the tap, we exercise faith that the water supply is safe. When we put faith in those terms, we must ask ourselves whether we daily exercise more faith in our society and economy, or in Jesus. This is the type of belief/faith to which Jesus referred.

In the case of the disciples, they were men who had exercised tremendous faith. They had left jobs, houses, and families in order to follow Jesus. It is clear that they believed they could cast out demons, because they already had. It appears that they did not shrink back when this man brought the boy. Further, he did not imply that they would not be able to cast it out. So, what was the problem?

Have you ever noticed that Jesus expected the disciples to do things that were impossible for them to accomplish? In years past, I kind of thought Jesus was being too hard on the disciples. I thought this way because I understood little about living in supernatural power. Jesus expected his disciples to feed the five thousand with five loaves and two fish. Then he gave them another chance with the four thousand, seven loaves, and a few fish. Both times, they struggled. Jesus expected the disciples to calm the storm. He expected Peter to keep walking on the water and not sink. Jesus expected his disciples to have faith to live supernatural, transformational lives. The disciples had experience casting out demons, but this incident was a new challenge; although they had cast out demons in the past, they could not depend on that experience for the power. They had to depend on heaven's power to cast out the demon. Have you ever noticed that when we gain a certain level of experience, we begin to depend on that past experience? We tell ourselves that we've done that before, so we can do it again. Often that is enough, but when we face a new and unprecedented challenge, we need more. Although Jesus did not explain this in detail, I think this is what happened. The disciples faced a situation that required them to have increased faith in Father's power to defeat the demonic, but they depended on their past, now inadequate, success in casting out demons.

While we have access to the necessary resources to win every battle in Jesus, we need to go to heaven to get them (Mark 9:20-24). Jesus calls us to live like the merchant of Matthew 13:45-46. Did the man have enough to purchase the pearl? Yes and no. He had enough, but he had to sell his house, his possessions, and his business to purchase it. He had access to the resources to purchase the pearl, but he didn't have them with him. He had to go get them. The disciples had access to the power needed to cast out the demon, but they had to go to heaven to get it, not their past experience. We have access to live supernatural lives, but we don't have that power on earth or in our past experience. We have to go to heaven to get it and apply it. Sometimes we just trust our own past victories for the power to have victory for new bigger challenges, rather than going to Father for help as we did in the past.

What do I mean? When we face a challenge for the first time, we pray, knowing that it is impossible. So, we go to Father for additional resources. He provides and we have victory. However, the next time, when we face a similar, but bigger challenge, we may just assume that since we already had victory, we can just move forward and not seek Father's resources—because we have already seen victory. I am coming to discover that the challenges in life are rarely just problems, but opportunities for connection with Father to have a co-victory over problems.

Furthermore, I find that often, my faith is limited to the natural and I rarely venture into the supernatural; I realize how little my faith is. For example, I seek God often for what I need to live, as in personal needs. What is ironic about that is Jesus promised all that in Matthew 6. Jesus said to seek the kingdom and all that you need will be given to you. If that is really true, why do I spend so much time seeking what I need materially? There is another problem. If I/we are so consumed about our personal needs, then who is pursuing heaven for the eradication of all disease? Who is seeking heaven to remove all crime and poverty? It occurs to me that my faith needs a significant upgrade. I need to focus on, not just my personal needs, but the needs of the kingdom.

This week, Donelle texted me and helped me understand the concept. As Americans, we often are influenced by the American dream, but I'm learning that I need to live for a higher dream—the Kingdom Dream. In this dream, we live for, not just personal prosperity, but kingdom prosperity.

Finally, how do we live in that reality? This is what Jesus referred to in his conclusion to the disciples. We get what we need through pursuing intimacy with God in worship and prayer (Mark 9:28-29). The disciples came to Jesus and asked him why they couldn't cast out the demon. Jesus responded, saying that demons of that type could only be cast out with prayer. Jesus' response is intriguing, because when Jesus cast out the demon, he did not pray. He didn't ask the Father to cast it out. He simply commanded the demon to leave and never return. Mark says that he rebuked the spirit. This is the same word that Jesus used when he rebuked the wind and the waves; when he rebuked Peter for opposing the way of the cross; when James and John wanted to call down fire on the Samaritan village. When they tried to cast out the demon, rebuking is probably what the disciples had done before, but without success. So, what did Jesus mean by saying that prayer was the only means of overcoming that demon?

I believe that we may get some indications from biblical examples of prayer. There is an attitude in prayer that Jesus taught, which we are invited/called to follow. I think of three examples, two from the New Testament

Living Out a Transformed Life • 117

and one from the Old Testament. In Matthew 15:21-28, Matthew told the story of a mother who came to Jesus for help. Jesus told her that it was not his mission to help her since she wasn't Jewish, but she came back for help anyway. Jesus again told her it wasn't correct for him to help her, but she would not take no for an answer. Jesus saw her great faith and healed her daughter. Like this woman, we at times face impossible situations. Jesus indicated that the impossibility does not mean a solution is not possible, but that we need to go to Father. However, there may be times when we must refuse to take "no" for an answer. In fact, we may mistake a seemingly negative response for a "no" and give up, when it is an invitation from Father to insist. Sometimes, we may give up just too early in prayer.

In Luke 18:1-8, Jesus told a parable with the purpose to teach us to persist in prayer. The widow needed the judge to give her justice. She would not relent until the judge did his job. It is interesting to note that she called him higher in order to fulfill who he was. A judge who does not give legal protection is a contradiction. In his refusal to help her, the judge was a living contradiction. Her persistence led to his fulfilling his own destiny. Jesus then warns us not to confuse God with the judge who delayed, because God will respond quickly to persistent prayer. Jesus concludes with a question. Will the Son of Man find faith on the earth when he comes? In other words, will Jesus find his people persisting in prayer when he comes, or simply giving up and living with the consequences?

Finally, an example from the Old Testament. In Exodus 32:10-14, Moses was on the mountain with God when the people chose the path of idolatry. God warned Moses to sit back and be quiet, but Moses disobeyed God and interceded for the people. He called upon God to remember his people and defend his testimony before the Egyptians. By wiping out Israel, the Egyptians would say that God only took them out into the desert to slaughter them. Make no mistake, Israel deserved God's judgment, but Moses appealed to God's mercy and his witness to the Egyptians. God heard Moses and chose to extend mercy to Israel. This is an amazing example of bold prayer to move the hand of God. If Moses had this type of influence with God, how much more do you and I have because we are in Christ and seated in the heavenlies?

Finally, we need to look at what prayer is, because too often we limit it. In the New Testament, there is not just one word that is translated into English by our word "prayer." Sometimes the word translated as "prayer" in English is the Greek word "ask," sometimes the word is "supplicate," and sometimes the word is "intercede." This particular word was the word that we read when Jesus referred to the temple as a "house of prayer," or when Jesus spent a night in "prayer." Our English word, "prayer," emphasizes meanings like supplicate, intercede, or sometimes even beg. However, this word also includes the concept of "worship." I believe that Jesus referred to a type of prayer which is more than a list of requests made to God, but involves communion and worship in the presence of God. The verb form of the word here is used in 1 Thessalonians 5:17, where Paul instructed us to pray without ceasing. If we view prayer as only making requests of God, this is difficult to do while we are working, while we are at school, while we are driving, or while we are watching a sporting event. However, if we grasp the reality that prayer is also living in heaven's reality—with a conscious recognition that the Spirit is with us and that we are seated with Christ in the heavenlies—it's a whole different perspective.

It's a bit like this. Donelle and I like watching movies together. While we may not be interacting, we are each conscious of one another's presence. During the movie, we may make comments to one another. I believe Jesus lived his life like this in relationship to the Father through the presence of the Spirit in his life. This is how we are to live our lives. We are to live with a constant awareness of the spiritual, heavenly world—which is unseen—but is more real than the natural world, because it is eternal. Jesus called us to live with a constant awareness of his presence.

Questions for Reflection

1. How might have past successes in your life limited opportunities for further growth?
2. How might you see your faith move from intellectual belief to life transformation?
3. Consider some ways to increase your awareness of Jesus' constant presence with you.

TEN

Living Out Kingdom Greatness

RECENTLY, the Holy Spirit has been teaching me again that kingdom living is very different than the world's way of living. Following Jesus is so different than living the "normal" American life. I believe it's for this reason that Jesus gave instruction to his followers on how they were to live in the world. He not only taught us, but he also lived out himself how we were to live. One area of contrast between kingdom living and the world's way of living is in the area of greatness. How the world views greatness and how the kingdom defines greatness are drastically different.

How does the world define greatness? Great men and women are people who do "great" things. They have made great accomplishments and become known. They are recognized for their efforts. They worked hard and, because of their hard work, they became famous. Greatness seems to be more about becoming known, because there are many who work very hard their entire lives and are never called "great" by the world. In sports, the great are those who get elected to their sport's Hall of Fame. In politics, they are the ones that historians write about, including the legacy they left. As great men and women, they are usually rewarded with honors, position, and wealth. In many of us, if not all of us, there is something that yearns to be great. We want to do something significant. We want to leave a legacy. We want to be remembered for having made a difference.

Therefore, it is not surprising to read that Jesus' disciples talked about being great. Jesus never said it was wrong to desire greatness; rather he defined what greatness is in the kingdom. Apparently, the disciples were somewhat embarrassed about having discussed greatness, because Mark tells us that they were silent when Jesus asked them about what they had been discussing. It is ironic that, while men and women desire greatness, they can be embarrassed about desiring it. Again, this is distortion from the world. Father, like any good father, desires us to be great. However, he desires us to pursue greatness as he defines greatness, not as the world defines greatness.

Since the desire to be great is in us, we should talk about it. We should not deny or ignore our divinely given desire to be great; we must develop it in terms of our Father's kingdom. That is what Jesus did. He revealed to his disciples what kingdom greatness is.

To reveal kingdom greatness, Jesus used a young child as an example (Luke 9:46-48). The fact that Jesus could immediately take a child and have him/her at his side reveals that he lived with children constantly around him. Just that fact is revealing of Jesus' greatness. While the disciples shooed children away, Jesus welcomed them and often had children in his presence. Some people view children as an annoyance. They are to be seen, but not heard. Some see children as a distraction, because they require time and attention. Scripture calls children a blessing, but some don't see children in that light. In contrast to the disciples, Jesus welcomed children. He desired for them to be around him and made sure they were close by.

On another occasion, Jesus revealed an amazing truth about children (Matthew 19:13-15). They are the living revelation of kingdom citizens. When the disciples hindered parents from bringing children into his presence, Jesus rebuked them, telling the disciples to stop hindering them. He said the kingdom belongs to those who come like children. Children are a portrait of kingdom citizenship. They own nothing; they don't worry about tomorrow; they enjoy what they have in the present; they believe that their parents will provide for them, and they laugh exponentially more than adults. Living in the kingdom is supposed to be like that. Over and over, Jesus told us to focus on the kingdom, on the Father's will, and on Jesus' will to completely take care of us.

Jesus went on to describe how the disciples were to treat children (Luke 9:48). The Greek word, "dechomai," is not the most common for "receive," but it is used over fifty times in the New Testament. It has the connotation of "willingly accepting or even taking." This word is almost always used to describe how someone positively (or negatively) responded to Jesus, the disciples, or the gospel. It implies accepting something that is offered to you. Jesus tells us that we are to willingly accept children as if they were Jesus himself.

Then, Jesus shifted the point slightly. First, he said that those who receive a child receive him or her and the

Father. Then, he said that the least are the greatest in the kingdom. Jesus implied that, not only are we to warmly receive the childlike, but we become great when we become like them. I think of the passage where Jesus said that those who receive (dechomai) a prophet also receive his reward (Matthew 10:41). In our warm reception of children, we also receive their reward, the kingdom of God. According to Jesus, we are not just talking about greatness in the kingdom, we are talking about entrance into the kingdom. We are to be like children.

To clarify, this does not mean we are to be childish, but we are to be humble like children who are perfectly comfortable being in a needy state and recognize their need of help from those who are bigger and stronger than they are. Paul voluntarily did this when he said he had considered all of his accomplishments as trash in comparison to knowing Jesus (Philippians 3:7-8). All of our abilities and accomplishments are not the foundation for greatness; the foundation for greatness is the blessings of God upon our lives.

Children trust. They believe what adults tell them. Do you know what we call adults when they have childlike trust? When adults believe what others tell them without question, we call them naive and say they should "grow up." This is just one way that the world has robbed us of our joy and peace in Jesus. Growing up, we learn and are taught that we cannot always trust others, which is true, but then we mistakenly believe that we cannot trust Jesus either. Jesus told us to be "converted" and become like children. In so doing, we must trust Jesus alone to protect us. In many ways, learning to mature in Jesus is unlearning what it means to be an adult in western society.

Jesus says that those of the kingdom will be fundamentally different from those of the world. The world tends to arrange relationships around a "what's in it for me" paradigm, while the kingdom arranges relationships around a "what can I do for you" paradigm. Kingdom citizens live with this latter paradigm, because they know they have great value in the sight of the Father. In the parallel passage in Mark, Jesus reminded the disciples that the one who is great in the kingdom is the one who seeks to serve and is not concerned about recognition or position (Mark 9:35). In the world, people jockey to be recognized and promoted, but in the kingdom, people look for how they can make a difference by serving.

In Luke 9, Jesus indicated that the way we relate to and treat children is an indicator of our relationship with Jesus. Also, how we treat all those who are child-like is an indicator of our relationship with Jesus. The truth is that children have the greatest faith of anyone. The child-like are those who, as they grow up, don't allow their faith in Jesus to be educated out of them by intellectual and materialistic educational systems. In the world, children and the child-like are tolerated, but not highly valued because they are not viewed as individuals who have much to offer. The child-like are often not well connected and are likely not great at helping you much in achieving your goals. They are not very good at "you scratch my back and I'll scratch yours" method of doing business. Often, all they have to offer is relationship, which is significant and foundational in the kingdom, but valued by few, because most are looking for some advantage from their relationships. Again, this is contrary to how Jesus instructed us to live. He told us to expend our energy on those who do not have the resources to "promote" us, because then it will be our heavenly Father to lift us up. How different is Jesus' description of greatness than the normal standards of greatness? By this statement, Jesus, without saying it, told us what greatness is not.

Greatness does not come from education.

Greatness does not come from teaching right doctrine and possessing biblical knowledge.

Greatness does not come from noteworthy accomplishments.

Greatness will likely never be recognized by the world.

Greatness does not come from having wealth.

Jesus went on to further define kingdom greatness as not creating barriers where none exist (John 9:49-50). John and the disciples seemed to practice something that many religious people do. A man was using Jesus' name to set others free, but since he did not belong to their group, John and the disciples forbade him from doing so. Jesus told them to not forbid individuals like that. As I looked into the word, "forbid," I discovered a curious phenomenon. I assumed that the word would have been used in the New Testament for God forbidding us to do sin or evil. However, it is never used in that manner. In the Gospels, the word translated here as "forbid" is only used in the same manner that we see here. Men with their rules and traditions are "forbidding" each other from doing good things. It is used here; it was also used in the passages regarding children when Jesus told the disciples to stop hindering the parents from bringing their children. On one occasion, Jesus was falsely accused of forbidding the paying of taxes to Caesar. Contrary to what we may have believed, we find Jesus telling his disciples to stop forbidding people from certain actions. I found this a fascinating lesson on "forbidding." I discovered that, often, we are much more concerned about making sure others follow rules than Jesus seems to be.

Since early in church history, we have forgotten what Jesus said here. We have tended to build unity around common beliefs and common doctrine. Then we "forbid" others from being part of our community if they do not follow our recognized list of doctrines. Since the Reformation, we have called them "denominations."

I used to teach that denominations were merely different expressions of the church. I don't believe that any longer. I have come to believe that denominations have unnecessarily divided the church, because we have placed an unnecessary emphasis on doctrine to the exclusion of relationship with others who love Jesus. Historically, Christians have drawn lines of agreement and consequently created division that Jesus didn't establish or that was not established in Scripture. For example, Christians have divided over who Jesus is, what baptism is, how you receive eternal life, who the Holy Spirit is, when you receive the Holy Spirit, what the Bible is, how old the earth is, what the future holds, etc. However, Scripture teaches that, to enter into the kingdom, we only need to believe that Jesus is physically alive and confess him as Lord (Romans 10:17). Romans 10:17 leaves a lot of room for divergent understanding of the Bible, while at the same time maintaining unity. It is somewhat ironic that we Christians have become more restrictive regarding the kingdom than Jesus is. Historically, Christians believed that only those who were part of their group were the ones who should be operating in Jesus' name. Jesus corrected the disciples here, suggesting that we should also reconsider our practices. In the early chapters of Acts, the church believed that only devout Jews could enter into the kingdom. Jesus corrected this, first through Peter (Acts 10-11) and later Paul (Galatians).

Jesus warned against such sectarian approaches to the kingdom. In Mark, he elaborated, saying that those who operate in his name are not against you. Just because someone isn't part of our group does not mean he or she doesn't belong to Jesus. If that person belongs to Jesus, then we can and should welcome him/her as a brother or sister in Jesus' name. In other words, what unifies Christians is not doctrinal agreement, but a relationship with Jesus. Insisting on doctrinal agreement has tended to divide followers of Jesus rather than unite them. Consider how divided Christians are in the world today. In 1054, the east (Greek) and west (Roman) divided over doctrines regarding how to worship and who's in charge. In the Reformation, Europe divided north and south over how sins are forgiven and church authority. The Reformation churches divided over communion, baptism, and how you become a Christian. In the last hundred years, Christians have divided over the Bible, the Holy Spirit, baptism, tongues, spiritual gifts, and when to worship, to name a few; but at the same time, everyone claims to love Jesus.

We seem to have forgotten that you can be united in relationship, but still disagree over other matters. Many of us work every day with people and we have relationships with them, but we may disagree with them over many important issues; yet we still cooperate with them, care about what happens to them, and spend our days at work with them. How come people, some of whom don't know Jesus, can be united without agreement, but the church, who claims to follow Jesus and claims to have the Holy Spirit, does not operate in agreement? Perhaps we have forgotten what Jesus said here.

Rather than focusing on our disagreements or ignoring them, it seems wiser to ask a simple question. What led someone who loves Jesus to come to a different conclusion about following him? As we discover the reasons, we can learn more about ourselves. This is what children do. They constantly observe others and learn. As adults, we tend to think we've learned everything and are often only looking for better arguments to defend what we've already concluded. This attitude seems to run counter to what Jesus taught. Kingdom greatness leaves open the possibility for growth and change. Growth and change imply that what we currently understand may not be completely accurate.

Jesus' words to John and the other disciples reveal that kingdom power (supernatural power) is to be used for good, not for destruction (Luke 9:51-56). It is curious to consider the reality that, in many people's perspective, Christians are more known for what they are against than for being a blessing. In the last 100 years, Christians have become known for being against alcohol, movies, dancing, rock music, smoking, abortion, immorality, and lately, human trafficking. While it is important that we stand up for what we believe is right, I have to wonder why we are not known more for being a blessing to society? The early Christians were known for caring for the sick and dying of Rome during epidemics. In the summer months, the ancient Romans fled to the sea or the mountains from epidemics, but Christians remained in the city to care for those dying of malaria and other diseases. They were known for taking in the baby girls that the Roman families abandoned. While the early Christians were persecuted by the Roman government, that same government recognized that they were a blessing.

In Luke 9, Jesus told the disciples to feed the five thousand. Jesus gave them the go-ahead to be a blessing, but they said that they could not. Yet, when they were offended by the Samaritans' refusal to receive them, James and John were ready to use their kingdom authority to destroy the village. I find that an odd contrast. Why, when invited to use kingdom power to bless, did they have no faith, but when they wanted to use kingdom power to destroy, they had all the faith in the world? Jesus warned them about the spirit that had provoked them to that attitude which used power for destruction. James and John thought they were protecting Jesus, but Jesus rebuked them. When we use our authority to curse those who disagree with us or live in a manner contrary to the kingdom, we are operating outside the heart of Father.

Nevertheless, Jesus continued to reveal that Father is for us. He taught us that Father wants us to live like Jesus lived, completely focused on kingdom business and not on our material needs. This is our divine partnership. We occupy ourselves with Father's business, bringing kingdom blessing to the world, and Father promises to provide everything we need to live our life. However, we tend to focus our time and energy on getting our physical and emotional needs met and occupying ourselves with the kingdom in our spare time. This is opposite to how

Jesus taught us to live, and I find a subtle lie at the heart of this confusion of focus. The lie is that Father is not really for me; that he will let me down, so I have to take care of myself. What I find strange about this lie is that it has absolutely no substance in reality. While I've experienced disappointment in life, I cannot say that Father has ever abandoned me or let me down. Yet, I do battle with that lie.

This is what Jesus indicates here. Kingdom greatness means that we rediscover Jesus' practice of standing for what is right, while at the same time using our kingdom authority to bless all those around us. As we do so, we refuse to be distracted by our own physical and material needs, because we live with daily confidence that our Father will provide for us.

Jesus gives us permission to love those who love him but have come to different conclusions about doctrine. We don't have to force people to believe all the things that we do, or to live like we do. As Paul said, we are to live with only the debt of love to others.

Questions for Reflection

1. How can children teach you to live more closely to Father?
2. How have doctrine or denominational differences impacted how you relate to other followers of Jesus?
3. In what ways would those who know you conclude that you love Jesus?

ELEVEN

Applying Kingdom Greatness

ONE OF THE important aspects in life is mission. At our former church, New Horizons Church in McMinnville, Oregon, the mission is three-fold: be a church of presence, enable others for kingdom living, and expand the kingdom. All of us who know Jesus have a similar purpose. Through knowing Jesus, we've been called to know Father (presence). This is also reflected in the great commandment to love God with all your heart. Then, we are all called to equip others. This calling is reflected in the new commandment that Jesus gave, to love as he has loved us (John 13:33-35). By the way, this was a new commandment, because it was greater than what Jesus had previously called the second commandment, to love your neighbor as yourself. It is both newer and greater, because Jesus loves you and me more than we love ourselves; therefore, our love for others is to be even greater than our love for ourselves. Finally, we are called to expand the kingdom, revealed in the great commission. Since Jesus has all authority, we are to make disciples of all peoples and ethnic groups existent in the world (Matthew 28:18-20). These are our purposes. Sometimes we need to refocus, because our purpose is not an education, career success, business success, ministry success, marriage success, or family success. It is not having enough money to live comfortably. We may receive these things, and they are good, but they are tools for achieving our kingdom purpose.

In the previous chapter, we looked at what it meant to be great in the kingdom, as well as how we are to become childlike and receive others as if they were Jesus himself. In this chapter, we will see how kingdom greatness is lived out in the world. As an example to us, we are given the story of Jesus sending the seventy out to the cities ahead of him to proclaim the kingdom. We must realize that this is also our mission. Jesus sends us into the world ahead of him. He said he was coming back. That means we are like John the Baptist, sent ahead of Jesus to prepare all peoples for Jesus' return.

People are hungry for Jesus. After almost thirty years in full time Christian ministry, I had forgotten how fascinating it is to work out in the world. What I enjoy most is the people. I enjoyed teaching Italian; however, it wasn't so much teaching Italian, but the friendship I developed with my student. What I enjoy about working in the home improvement business is my colleagues there. People in the world are searching. They know deep down that there has to be more than what they have. We have the answer. Jesus said that the harvest is plentiful; it is true. People need to know that we care for them, because Father loves them.

The point is that our work environment is the context

for us to show others how much they are loved and appreciated. I look around and see how many people are working seven days a week, sometimes 12-15 hours a day. They have little or no down time. They live that way because they think that is what they need to do to be fulfilled or happy. For many, their only refuge is some diversion from the weariness of their daily life. Jesus tells us that we are to lay down our yoke, our burden, and take up his (Matthew 11:28-29). The lie that often creeps in is that Jesus' yoke is heavy, but his yoke is actually a relief. Jesus said his yoke was light. We are to trade the heavy yoke that is driving us to work too hard and wears us out; we are much harder taskmasters for ourselves than Jesus is. However, the lie persists that Jesus and Father are severe.

Kingdom greatness is lived out as we help people understand that our care for them is actually a reflection of Father's love for them. Our goal is not achievement, business success, wealth, or recognition; these are the context to open doors for us to reveal Jesus to people who desperately need him.

On the other hand, apparent lack is not an actual reflection of the power and authority you possess. Jesus described his disciples, and also us, as lambs living out in a world of wolves (Luke 10:3-6). Being lambs surrounded by wolves is a dangerous environment. Why did Jesus say that? Although we may appear as lambs, we are not without protection. The lamb is always safe in the face of wolves when the shepherd is there protecting him. David grasped this truth in Psalm 23 when he said that the Lord (Yahweh) was his shepherd. When David declared the Lord as his shepherd, he also declared that he himself was a lamb, because lambs are the ones for whom shepherds care. David added that the Lord prepared a table for him in the presence of his enemies. Who are the enemies of lambs, but wolves? I assure you wolves always know where the lambs are, and they watch for an opportunity to strike, but they cannot because the shepherd is there. They will never attack when the shepherd is present. This is important for us to remember. Jesus does send us out as lambs into a land of wolves, but he does not send us out without protection, because he is with us in the person of the Holy Spirit.

In the Great Commission, Jesus told the disciples to go out and make disciples of all nations, and then he added that he would always be with them until the end of the age (Matthew 28:18-20). If Jesus is with us, then we are not alone. If Jesus is with us, then we are protected. Even though we face those who appear stronger and more powerful than us, we will succeed.

At the end of Mark, we read a description of Jesus' protection over his disciples. He says that they will go out with accompanying signs: they will cast out demons, they will not be hurt by serpents or poison, and they will lay hands on the sick who will be healed (Mark 16:17-18). Some discount this passage, because it is not found in all of the New Testament manuscripts. That is true; however, what is quoted in Mark 16 is confirmed in the book of Acts. The disciples did everything that Jesus said in these verses. So, whether or not this passage is in Mark is beside the point. The point is that Jesus does protect his own whom he sends out into a world filled with opposition. His protection of them and his power displayed through them is a testimony to the world, because everyone knows that lambs are weak and powerless in and of themselves.

Furthermore, Jesus instructed his disciples not to take wealth with them. I do not believe that this is an absolute rule, because later Jesus said that the disciples were to take provisions for themselves. I believe this was a lesson they needed to learn. Jesus would and could provide for them, even when it appeared that they didn't have anything (Luke 22:35-37). The problem is never wealth, success, recognition, or possessions; the problem is always our dependence on them and when we place our faith in them. We are called to live consistent lives. If we lack, we are to trust Jesus. If we have an abundance, we are to trust Jesus. This is true, because worldly wealth is temporal and fragile. It can be here one day and gone the next. If our faith is in our possessions, our faith is fragile because fear of losing our possessions can rise up and take control of us. However, if our trust is in Jesus, then we can accept the fragility of life, knowing that our wealth is in heaven.

What Jesus gives to us is greater than all the wealth, power, and possessions the world offers; he offers us peace. If you have all that the world offers but do not have peace, you have nothing. Jesus asked, "what good is it for someone to gain the whole world, yet forfeit their soul?"

At times he couldn't heal, like in Nazareth. Other times, he told people not to tell anyone what had happened until the proper time. In his instruction here, Jesus told the disciples to heal in the places that received them. Healing seems to most often take place in those who desire more of Jesus and not in those who are resistant to an increase of him. This is what Jesus pointed out here. In the places the disciples were received, people were healed. However, in those places where they were not received, they were not even to take with them any dust that clung to their feet when they left. For as these people rejected the kingdom, so one day they would be judged.

Nevertheless, consider the cities that Jesus rebuked. They were not the cities that rejected him, like Nazareth. They were the cities in which he did the major part of his teaching and healing. Bethsaida was where Peter, Andrew, and Philip came from. The citizens of Bethsaida chased after Jesus. Yet, he rebuked them. Why? They didn't repent. From what? In John 6:26, Jesus rebuked the people for their desires. Yes, they followed Jesus, but not to be transformed. Rather, they only wanted to have their physical needs met. For them, Jesus was an investment strategy to improve their life. Jesus told them to seek eternal life. The disturbing aspect of Jesus' words is that he had such harsh words toward people who were both religious and appeared to follow him. However, history teaches us that traditional followers of God tend to be resistant to new works of God. Jesus represented a new work of God, but the religious Jews tended to oppose him.

If we consider Jesus' teaching here, what does this say about our nation? Why do we see revival in other parts of the world, but not here at the same level? It strikes me how so many with the gifts of healing tell us that they do not see miracles taking place here as they see them taking place in parts of Asia, South America, and Africa. Is it possible that we have believed a lie which subtly causes us to reject Jesus just like Bethsaida, Chorazin, and even Capernaum? Christians love to take pride in declaring that the United States is a Christian nation, founded upon Christian principles. Some years ago, when President Obama made the statement that the United States was not a Christian nation, many Christians took offense. However, have we ever considered that God may have been revealing a lie to us through an unexpected source?

Although historically, we have been a nation that professes Christian principles and religion, there are disturbing, violent, and brutal aspects of our history that do not reflect a nation founded on Christian principles and one living for the kingdom. Native Americans are often resistant to the gospel because of how they've been treated. We don't have a very close relationship with Mexico, partly because of how things worked out in the Mexican-American War. Even the First Great Awakening didn't have the transforming impact in the United States that it did in Britain. Historically, our foreign policy has been more of a "might makes right," which is not reflective of a Christian nation. President Theodore Roosevelt, not Jesus, said, "speak softly and carry a big stick." If the United States were a Christian nation, it would accurately reflect Jesus. When people reject Jesus because of the non-Jesus-like way our "Christian" nation has treated them, then we must take responsibility. So why do we take offense when our President declares the obvious to anyone who has studied American history? Might it be because we've believed a lie and not taken a close look at our national history? Might our refusal as followers of Jesus to repent from our national sins hinder us from receiving more as a nation from our Father who desires to give us more?

Nevertheless, our joy comes not from kingdom success, but from intimacy with Jesus. The seventy returned with an amazing testimony of victory. If we had been there, we would have cheered the results. Who wouldn't? People were set free from the demonic. Jesus said he had come to set the captives free, and the seventy were part of the fulfillment of Jesus' proclamation. Their ministry had a kingdom impact, because Jesus declared that he had seen Satan fall from heaven like lightning. Satan's power was diminished through the seventy going out and declaring the kingdom, declaring peace and healing, and setting people free.

Jesus summarized their authority. They had authority over all the power of the enemy, and nothing would injure them. The word "injure" seems to say that, although Christians face evil, it cannot have any lasting effect upon them. The word "injure," in Greek, is also translated as "being wronged" in the New Testament. At times, it can refer to physical injury, but most often, it has the meaning of being wronged. In any case, Jesus declared to the seventy that they were the ones who had the upper hand, not the god of that age, for he has been defeated.

All this causes us to rejoice, but then Jesus added a reminder. As wonderful as it is to experience spiritual victory and to see the sick healed, the prisoners set free, and the kingdom of God expanded on earth, this is not to be the source or cause of our joy. We are to be joyful because of relationship; we belong to Jesus, and therefore, our names are written in heaven. Jesus' words should not surprise us, for the truly joyful on earth are those who enjoy relationship, not necessarily those recognized for success. We all know people who have been successful in various ventures but struggle nonetheless. Consider Evan Roberts, the young man through whom God brought the Wales Revival and from which sprang the Azusa Street Revival in Los Angeles. Roberts spent the majority of his life disillusioned and in seclusion. Even relationships with his family were strained. We may struggle to understand how this could happen, but his story reveals that discouragement is possible, even among those through whom revival comes. Even an extremely successful life on earth can be unsatisfying if a void of relationship with Jesus also exists. Our joy is founded in relationship with Jesus, just as Jesus' joy was rooted in his relationship with Father.

Questions for Reflection

1. How does Jesus indicate that we are to live out kingdom greatness?
2. What do you find to be the most surprising aspects of Jesus' instruction to the seventy?
3. In what ways can you determine if your joy is coming from having your name written in heaven and not from ministry success?

TWELVE

Striving in the Right Way

MOST OF THE time when we read the Bible in English, the meaning is straight forward. The English word means exactly what was originally communicated in Hebrew or Greek. However, occasionally, we come across words that have different meanings in other languages, so it can be hard to translate them with just one word in English. To take a modern example, the English use of the Italian word "piano" means a musical instrument with white and black keys. However, in Italian, "piano" can mean: a musical instrument, level, flat, shelf, slow, soft, or quiet.

In the New Testament, sometimes there are words that have a variety of meanings, and if we are not aware of those meanings, we can become confused. That truth occurred to me recently when I read what Jesus said to his disciples in Luke 13:24-30 to strive to enter the narrow gate. What did Jesus mean when he said "strive" to enter through the narrow gate? Did he mean work at it? Not really, because we are told that we are saved by grace and not by works (Ephesians 2:8-9). Obviously, Jesus' teaching here is worth noting, because he explained to his disciples that they had to strive to enter the kingdom (the narrow door). And what could be more important than entering into the kingdom? So, it is imperative to understand what Jesus meant by "strive" to enter the narrow gate.

In this chapter, I want to do two things. I want to look at what it means to strive, but first I want to look at what Jesus said here about what we are to strive for—to enter through the narrow gate. What Jesus says here is troubling to me. Have you ever noticed that Jesus often said things that may be easy to gloss over, but as you reflect upon them, they are quite troubling?

Many seek to enter through the narrow gate but do not actually enter in (Luke 13:24). Many even think they have entered, only to discover they have not. What Jesus said in Luke 13 is very similar to what he said in Matthew 7:13-23. Again, he told his disciples to enter through the narrow gate. Then he went on to say that many would come to him having called him "Lord," having prophesied in his name, and having cast out demons in his name; yet, they do not know Jesus. In other words, there will be many people who have assumed that they had entered because they have been in Jesus' presence, because they have prophesied, because they have cast out demons; yet, they do not know Jesus and do not belong in the kingdom. It is a mystery how this can take place, but we have to take Jesus' words seriously. The people he refers to ate and drank with him; he taught in their streets, and they imitated Jesus, but Jesus did not know them. In both Matthew 7 and Luke 13, Jesus emphasized the relational aspect of the kingdom.

When I was little, the Green Bay Packers' coach was Vince Lombardi, and the Packers were known for being great. In the off season, a number of the players would travel around the state of Wisconsin to meet fans and promote the team. Whenever these events took place in the town where I grew up, my parents took me. I met the players, got their autographs, and shook their hands. I told them my name. In other words, I was in their presence. However, I could not say that they knew me or that I knew them. I believe this is what Jesus says here. It is possible for us to hang around places where Jesus shows up; it is possible to imitate Jesus; it is possible for us to even see Jesus; it is possible for us to know people who know Jesus, but never to actually know him ourselves. Jesus indicates that knowing him is of utmost importance. So, the word, "strive," here must have some connection with entering into a relationship with Jesus in which we know him and he knows us.

Furthermore, being religious is not the same as knowing Jesus (Luke 13:26). In this context, Jesus seems to be addressing the false assumption that the religious people of his day were close to God. In Luke 13:31-35, Jesus went on to address the Pharisees along with the city of Jerusalem, warning them about their future. Jerusalem was the most religious city of the Jews, but it was also one that often opposed Jesus and God the Father. That was Jesus' warning to the religious people of his day, but what is the lesson for today? It is not enough to be part of a church and to live a moral life; we must enter into a relationship with Jesus. And being in relationship with Jesus is more than responding to an invitation and praying a prayer.

It has occurred to me that I often underestimate the value of wilderness experiences. Typically, my wilderness experiences bring me to a place of knowing Jesus better. It is in the wilderness that I find myself pursuing his presence, power, and deliverance. It is often the battle in the wilderness that gives purpose to my life as I see his power revealed. If it were not for the wilderness, my life would be comfortable, but rather boring. While we desire to go from "glory to glory" (2 Corinthians 3:18), we cannot go from glory to glory without going from "wilderness to wilderness." Glory is often preceded by a wilderness experience. It occurred to me that there is a connection between the depth of the wilderness and the subsequent glory/victory that follows. It also occurred to me that in the wilderness, I tend to pursue Jesus, but in the victory, I tend to focus on the victory. This truth causes me to wonder why I have such a distaste for my wilderness experiences if those are the times when I am closest to Jesus. Why do I enjoy the fulfillment of his promises, and the exit from the wilderness, when it was during those times that I drew close to Jesus? Then, when I've exited the wilderness and am more comfortable, I don't pursue Jesus with the same intensity that I did during the wilderness. I find this both ironic and disturbing.

This leads us to what it means to strive. We've already seen that it does not necessarily mean "work" in the common sense of earning something. At this point, it is important to look at how the word is used in other places. In Scripture, when I try to find out what a word means, I look to see how it is used in other places.

Biblical striving is connected to our faith relationship with Jesus. We are to strive according to faith and fight the good fight of the faith (1 Timothy 6:12). This verse is found in the midst of Paul's instruction to Timothy on what to say to those tempted to seek after worldly wealth. Paul touches here one of the main contrasts in the kingdom. The world teaches us to evaluate reality according to our observations. A foundational observation is that if a person has wealth, health, and wisdom, then he is blessed by God. This is an accurate observation, but the problem comes in the conclusion. This is where Paul gave Timothy the warning. No one is to love the things in this world, for doing so will lead to destruction (1 Timothy 6:10; 1 John 2:15-17). Paul went on to explain why. We are not to place our hope in wealth, because it is uncertain (1 Timothy 6:17). Jesus added another reason that wealth can tend to capture our heart. He told us to invest our treasure in heaven, because where our treasure is, our heart will be (Matthew 6:20-21).

We know that wealth's uncertainty is true. In the 1990s, the talk was of the "new economy," because of the emergence of the dot-com industry. However, in 2000-2001, that sector collapsed. People who still had money left began to invest in real estate. That lasted until 2007-2008 when the real estate bubble burst. If anyone should know the uncertainty of material wealth, it should be us. The last twenty years have confirmed what Paul taught Timothy.

How about health? In Italy, we heard over and over that if you had your health, you had everything. However, we all know that at some point in time, our health will fail and we will die. Health is not a secure investment either. How about wisdom? While wisdom is a blessing, it comes with a price. Solomon pointed out that with increased knowledge/wisdom comes increased pain. If we are not to strive for wealth, or health, or wisdom, what are we to do? Paul tells us in 1 Timothy 6:11-12 that we are to strive for "righteousness, godliness, faith, love, perseverance and gentleness." The word "fight" in verse 12 is the same word translated as "strive," which Jesus used in Luke 13. We are to strive, fight, and contend for our faith relationship with Jesus, which leads to righteousness, godliness, and everything Paul mentioned in this passage. Even though the world bombards us with arguments to live for health, wealth, and wisdom, we are to focus our attention solely on Jesus and contend for our faith relationship with him.

That leads us to another question. How do we do this? I believe we develop our relationship with Jesus as we do any other relationship. Paul gave us a clue in Colossians 4:12. Biblical striving is done with prayer. In Colossians, Paul described one of the Colossians' own, Epaphras, who was with Paul and labored fervently through prayer on behalf of the Colossian church. It is extremely important that we understand what prayer is and what it is not. Religion turns prayer into a religious exercise or discipline. It was not that for Jesus. For Jesus, prayer was an opportunity for relationship. Prayer for Jesus was making a relational connection with his heavenly Father, which is exactly what we are to do. On earth, we can do things with our friends. However, with Jesus and our heavenly Father, we primarily connect with him through prayer.

An interesting phenomenon occurs when we spend significant amounts of time with someone. We tend to develop affection for that person. We grow to know them, appreciate them, and desire what is best for that person.

This is what happens when we begin to spend extended periods of time with Jesus in prayer. Now, understand when I speak of prayer, I also include worship, because I believe that worship is a form of prayer.

I think we can get some understanding about our spiritual relationship with Jesus through observing the way that marriage relationships tend to play out in our society. A couple gets together and has great affection for one another. They spend time together and enjoy being together. Since they enjoy one another so much, they decide to get married and commit to spending their lives together. Then, perhaps kids arrive, careers take off, and mortgages and car loans must be paid. At this point, if a couple doesn't continue to invest in their relationship, even though they've spent years doing all the right things, some split up about the time their last child heads off to college. Of course, some couples stay together, but they don't always enjoy being together all that much. They may go to marriage classes/counseling/seminars and learn all about resolving conflict and listening skills which, by the way, they didn't have when they were first married either; yet, they loved being together, nonetheless. They may learn all the right skills, do all the right things that the experts say you need to have a good marriage, and still not enjoy being together. Why? The foundation for marriage is affection for one another, and not necessarily skills. It is amazing how many couples love being together, even if they aren't really great listeners or communicators. Why? They have never lost affection for one another, but have cultivated it over the years. In the same way, we can do all the right Christian stuff: practice prophesy, do Bible study, attend church, serve others, heal the sick, and cast out demons. It is possible to do all these things because we are supposed to and still not have affection for Jesus or know him. This is the problem that I believe Jesus addressed. When Jesus meant strive to enter the kingdom, he meant we are to seek out and develop a genuine affection for him.

Many of us have been taught that in the New Testament, our word "love" is translated from several Greek words. If you've been around church for any length of time, you've probably heard sermons about agape love, which refers to a sacrificial type of love. For example, in John 3:16, the word "agape" is used. You may have also heard about "phileo" or "brotherly love," which is simply an emotional attachment to someone that we could translate with our word "affection." What you may not have heard is that God's love includes both agape and phileo. While in John 3:16, the word agape is used, Jesus said in John 5:20 that the Father loves the Son. In John 5:20, the word, phileo, is used. In John 16:27, Jesus said that the Father loves you because you have loved Jesus; again, the word used is not agape, but phileo. In other words, our love for Jesus needs to be both agape (sacrificial love) and phileo (affection) for Jesus. If we have only agape love, we tend to follow Jesus out of obligation or duty, which is religion and not relationship. We need to also develop our affection for Jesus.

When Jesus says to strive to enter the narrow gate, he refers to our making an effort to develop our relationship with him, which includes developing an affection for him. What does such striving look like? Let's look at examples.

Paul strove to know Jesus rather than seek earthly recognition (Philippians 3:1-21). In this passage, he gives to us an example of proper striving. In Philippians 3, Paul contrasted religious striving with true spiritual/biblical striving. Throughout his ministry, Paul had to deal with those who emphasized religious practices. In his case, it was the Jews who demanded that circumcision and following the Jewish ceremonial laws was foundational for growing close to God. However, Jesus fulfilled all those requirements so that we can draw close to Father through Jesus. As in Paul's day, even today there are sincere people who emphasize certain practices that they believe are necessary to be a Christian. Sometimes they are called theological distinctives that denominations emphasize.

Over the years, baptism, communion, church attendance, Bible study, and speaking in tongues have been taught and believed to bring spiritual growth and maturity in some denominations. While these are all good things, you can do all these things and still be relationally far from Jesus, even though you may appear to others as a mature Christian. This was Paul's point. From the outside, Paul could demonstrate that he participated in all those religious activities, so he was not opposed to their practice. He opposed the belief that they were necessary for salvation in Jesus or for entrance into the kingdom of God. Some people practice religion because they think they must establish their own righteousness; this is what Paul opposed. He taught that the only true righteousness is found in relationship with Jesus.

Paul went on to encourage the Philippians to follow his example, to imitate him, because he was constantly pursuing a deeper relationship with Jesus. Recently, a friend asked me what he needs to do to grow closer to Jesus. I told him to find people who have what he wants and to hang around them, because we become like those we hang around with. I told him to ask those he wants to imitate to pray for him and give to him what they have. We rub off on each other. Paul lived for a closer relationship with Jesus; this is what we need as well.

Sometimes we develop a close relationship with someone by going through difficulties together. Paul also had to endure difficult experiences himself. He spoke of one in 2 Corinthians 12. He called it a "messenger (angel) from Satan." I know that, regarding this passage, there is some controversy which we don't have time to address now. For our purposes, we need to look at what Jesus told Paul and Paul's response in 2 Corinthians 12:9-10. Jesus told Paul that his grace was sufficient for Paul and that Jesus' power is perfected in weakness. Our heavenly Father is not the author of what Paul endured in 2 Corinthians 12. Paul said that it was a messenger from Satan that caused him difficulty, not a messenger from Jesus. Nevertheless, in this world, we do see Jesus' power magnified in weakness; otherwise, how would we ever know that Jesus is powerful? When we are strong, we often don't seek or think we need Jesus' power, because we seem to be doing fine without it. It is only when we are weak that we see Jesus' power manifested most clearly in our lives. Since Paul had a great desire to know and love Jesus, this response more than satisfied him. Paul knew that his purpose in life was not comfort, but that the power of Jesus would dwell continually in him. If Paul had to be weak to accomplish that end, then not only would he accept it, but he would boast about it.

I believe Paul's teaching in 2 Corinthians 12 helps us understand the value of our wilderness experiences. He also reminds us that in weakness, Jesus' power in us is most evident. That should cause us to reflect a bit. Even though we do not know Paul's struggle, the word "weak" that is used here can mean physical illness and is sometimes translated with our English word, "infirmity." It can also mean some other form of weakness that is not necessarily physical. Paul's instruction in 2 Corinthians presents an interesting possibility. Often, we assume that when we are weak, we need to have others pray for us; but perhaps, when we are weak, we need to be the ones praying for others, because when we are weak, Jesus' strength is perfected in us.

Questions for Reflection

1. How would you describe the biblical concept of striving?
2. Why is it important to develop an affection for Jesus?
3. How can weakness and difficulty actually be blessings in our lives?

THIRTEEN

Father's Unfathomable Love for Us

AWHILE BACK, Donelle and I were watching a popular TV show about an empiricist and his friend who is Roman Catholic. The empiricist believed in only that which can be proven, and his friend used his faith and intuition to come to his conclusions. They were discussing what the empiricist called the "myth" of Abraham sacrificing Isaac. The Roman Catholic spoke of how he could never sacrifice his son for anyone. Those of us who are parents can perfectly understand his point. However, when I heard his statement, I began thinking about Abraham's decision in a completely different way. Listening to their conversation caused me to reflect further on this rather common story from Genesis, and it led me to some implications that I had never considered.

Typically, I have examined Abraham's decision to sacrifice Isaac as a stand-alone story. I had never considered what happened prior to that event. It occurred to me that this event was actually one in a series of emotional events in Abraham's life. So, before we look at Abraham's decision to sacrifice Isaac, let's take a look at what happened before that "test."

Genesis 21 begins with Isaac's birth, the fulfillment of the promise God had given to Abraham many years prior. It was a time of great joy. However, it also led to a series of emotional difficulties that Abraham would face and overcome. It is interesting to consider that, after the fulfillment of the prophecies declared to Abraham—when we think that everything would have been joyous and easy for him—the exact opposite took place. It is a reminder to us that, while we should pursue the fulfillment of prophetic words spoken to us, we must not think that once they are fulfilled, there are no other battles to face and win.

It is easy to look at Abraham's relationship with Ishmael and discount the emotion that he must have felt sending off his son into the wilderness. Even though Ishmael was not the son of promise, he was Abraham's son. We cannot just turn off the affection we feel for our children. Abraham must have felt a connection with Ishmael that Sarah clearly did not. To her, Ishmael was a distraction and possibly a threat, but to Abraham, he was a son. So understandably, Sarah's desire to send away Hagar and Ishmael was emotionally disturbing to Abraham; we would probably say that it broke his heart. Furthermore, God told Abraham that he should not feel disturbed, because Isaac was the child of promise, not Ishmael. I have to wonder how Abraham dealt with that conversation emotionally. Nevertheless, God promised to make Ishmael into a great nation, because he was Abraham's descendant. This seemed to give Abraham the encouragement and emotional strength to do what Sarah requested. What Abraham did sounds like someone else we know, but more of that later.

Immediately following what we read about Abraham sending Ishmael away, we read of a conflict that Abraham had with Abimelech and his commander. Abraham was forced to purchase what was already his in order to resolve the conflict. Abraham sacrificed what was his to establish peace with Abimelech, who claimed to be his friend. There is no little irony in this picture. Why should someone have to purchase what is already his? Sounds like someone else we know, but more of that later as well.

Finally, in Genesis 22, we come to the story of Abraham being tested by God, who asked him to sacrifice his son, Isaac. The word for test also has the meaning of tempt or prove. The Hebrew word "test" (nasa) is used primarily in two situations. God does prove his people, and it is appropriate. That is the meaning here with Abraham. It is used again in Deuteronomy 8, describing the wilderness experience and the manna. In the wilderness, God tested the heart of his people. It is used again in Deuteronomy 13 in reference to when the prophecies of false prophets came true, and the false prophets told the people to follow idols. It is also used in 2 Chronicles 32:31 to describe what happened to Hezekiah when the ambassadors from Babylon came. Scripture says that God left Hezekiah to test him and see what was in his heart.

Testing in this manner is the exclusive domain of God. It is legitimate for God to test and prove us to determine what is in our hearts as well. These tests do not mean that God is unaware of what is in our hearts. He is quite aware. These tests reveal what is in our hearts for both God *and* us to see. However, when man tests

God in this manner, it is always viewed as inappropriate. Our heavenly Father has already revealed to us what is in his heart; it is inappropriate for us to test him and prove his love for us. When Jesus quoted Deuteronomy 6:16, saying that we are not to put the Lord our God to the test, he was referring to this concept. This passage referred to an incident in Exodus 17:7—when the people tested the Lord in the manner of water, indicating their belief that the Lord had brought them out in the desert for them to die of thirst. When God's people desire that God prove himself, it is inappropriate and unnecessary.

However, in Malachi 3:10, when God says to test him by giving the tithe, a different word is used, "bahan." In that case, the word refers more to the testing of metal to reveal its purity. The words seem to indicate a difference between testing our Father's heart or character, which is inappropriate, and living according to a promise he has given and expecting him to honor it. The test is more for us to live according to what we've been promised, rather than testing God's truthfulness.

Returning to Genesis 22, God told Abraham to take his son Isaac, referring to him as his only son, which technically was not true biologically, but was true in terms of the promise and inheritance. God further described Isaac as the son Abraham loved. God had already told Abraham to remove Ishmael from his presence and inheritance. Abraham had endured a period of conflict with Abimelech, and now he was told to sacrifice his son of promise. Isaac represented all the fulfillment of the prophetic promises given to Abraham over the preceding decades. In telling Abraham to sacrifice Isaac, God was commanding him to not only sacrifice his son, but to sacrifice his future legacy and the promises that had been given to him.

It is important to note that Isaac was described with similar terminology that was used to describe Jesus: God's only begotten son and the son who was loved. After Jesus was baptized, Father declared from heaven that Jesus was his beloved son in whom he was well pleased (Matthew 3:17). This same declaration came from heaven again when Jesus was transfigured before Peter, James, and John, but with an addition—Father commanded the disciples to listen to Jesus (Matthew 17:5).

What is amazing about this account is indicated by what Abraham told the young men who had accompanied him and Isaac. Abraham said that they, Abraham, and Isaac would go and that they would return. Abraham believed that Isaac would be slain, burned on the altar, and then return with him. Although the term isn't used, resurrection is implied. This is what the author of Hebrews referred to when he wrote that Abraham believed that God was able to raise Isaac from the dead (Hebrews 11:19). When we read those words, we read them through the lens of Jesus' resurrection and numbers of other resurrection accounts recorded in Scripture. However, Abraham's case is fascinating, because prior to this point in Scripture, there is no record of anyone rising from the dead; yet, Abraham told those with him that he and Isaac would return, even though he had every intention to sacrifice Isaac in accordance with the command Father had given to him. Abraham believed that God would do something that had never been done before. When we pray for healing or raising someone from the dead, we are praying for something God has already done many times. We think that represents extraordinary faith, because we're praying for something supernatural, but Abraham believed God would do something that was both supernatural and had never been done before. His was an extraordinary faith; how might the world be different if we had faith like that of Abraham?

Further references to Jesus are seen here, such as when Abraham laid the wood of the sacrifice on Isaac's back. We are reminded of Jesus carrying his cross for a time until Simon was called to carry it to Golgotha. Genesis 22:8 reveals Abraham's faith, that God himself would provide a lamb for the sacrifice. This is the clearest reference to Jesus, who was referred to by John the Baptist as the lamb of God who takes away the sin of the world (John 1:29). Isaac was not literally sacrificed, but Jesus was. Isaac was not literally raised from the dead, but Jesus was.

When Abraham raised the knife to slay Isaac, God stopped him and revealed to him the test. God knew that Abraham feared (loved) God more than he loved Isaac. When we love someone, we are willing to sacrifice even that which is most dear to our hearts for them. Isaac was clearly dear to Abraham, yet Abraham's willingness to slay Isaac revealed his complete devotion to, trust in, and love for God. Not even his deep fatherly love for Isaac could stand in the way of his devotion to God. This is a powerful picture of love for God.

Since the Lord provided a ram to sacrifice instead of Isaac, Abraham called the place, "The Lord Will Provide." This location eventually became the place where Solomon would build the temple 1,500 years later, near to where Jesus would die on the cross. This story is filled with imagery of Jesus, as well as Abraham's faith in God.

The New Testament also sheds light on this event and puts it into context. The author of Hebrews draws some conclusions from the implications in Genesis 22. The author repeats that Abraham was tested, just as the Genesis story states. In Greek, the word is the normal word for tempt/test. This word is used in reference to both Satan and to God. When used of Satan's temptation of Jesus or us, it includes Satan's intent to destroy, but when used in reference to God, the intent is to approve.

The author of Hebrews described Abraham's thought process. Abraham seemed to believe that, since Isaac was the child of promise, he could not stay dead. Hebrews states what was implied in Genesis. Abraham believed that God would raise him from the dead. This is what Abraham believed God would do in regard to Isaac; this is also what God did in regard to his own son, Jesus. And through Jesus, all of Abraham's spiritual descendants would be named.

The account of Abraham sacrificing Isaac is much more than just a story about trusting God. While it is that, it is also a picture of our heavenly Father and Jesus. This story foreshadows what our heavenly Father would do with Jesus on the cross. So, we must also look at it in light of what Jesus did for us on the cross and what it communicates to us about Jesus' and Father's love for us. It leads to another important question. What does the "so loved" in John 3:16 really mean? To what extent does God love the world, so that he would slay his only begotten son on our behalf? We need to take some time to examine the extent of God's love for us.

Prior to his death, Jesus taught his disciples about love. Throughout John 15, he used the term, agape, which reflects sacrificial love. In verse 9, Jesus compared Father's love for him to Jesus' own love for his disciples. This is a powerful comparison. Why? Is there any greater love than Father's love for Jesus? We are inclined to say no, because Father is God and Jesus is God, so we assume that this is the greatest bond of love possible in all of creation. So, when Jesus says that he loves his disciples, then there is no greater love that can be extended toward you and me because all Christians are his disciples. Jesus confirmed this through the words in verse 13. He declared that there is no greater love than for a man to lay down his life for his friends. What is the point? This again is the truth of sacrifice. When Abraham was willing to sacrifice Isaac, his beloved son, he revealed to God that he loved God more than he loved Isaac. Now, when Jesus said that he was laying down his life for the disciples, he declared that he loved them even more than his own life. This is another confirmation of the truth of sacrifice.

We only sacrifice something for someone if we love that person more than whatever we sacrifice. If we love the sacrifice more, then we will not make the sacrifice. Our refusal to make the sacrifice means that we love the sacrifice more than the person. Let me give you an example.

In the story of the rich young ruler, we find another example of the principle of sacrifice (Luke 18:18-24). The ruler wanted to receive eternal life, so he inquired as to how he may receive it. Jesus told him to follow the law. The ruler already did. Then Jesus added that he needed to sell everything, give it to the poor, and follow Jesus. The man refused. Why did the man refuse? Because he loved his riches more than Jesus, so he refused to sacrifice them for Jesus' sake. His refusal to sacrifice reveals that he loved his wealth more than Jesus. If he had sacrificed his wealth and followed Jesus, then he would have revealed that he loved Jesus more than his wealth. This is why Jesus went on to say how hard it is for a rich person to receive eternal life, because the wealthy often love their wealth more than they love Jesus. Later on, in verse 28, Peter said that they had left everything to follow Jesus, meaning that they loved Jesus more than their wealth. Jesus affirmed Peter by saying that he would take care of Peter both in this world and in the world to come (18:30).

Jesus showed us that if we sacrifice something for someone, we love them more than what we sacrificed. Abraham revealed this principle when he was willing to sacrifice Isaac. Jesus revealed this when he laid down his life for us on the cross. The rich ruler demonstrated the opposite when he refused to sacrifice his money to follow Jesus. There was nothing more precious for Jesus to give than his own life. In this is the extent of Jesus' love for us. Now let's look at, perhaps, the best-known verse in the Bible, John 3:16, through the lens of Genesis 22.

God told Abraham to take his son Isaac, whom he loved, and sacrifice him (Genesis 22:1). Abraham was willing to do so and proved that his love for God surpassed even his own love for Isaac. John says that God loved the world so much, he gave his only begotten son for the world (John 3:16). Isn't it odd that people struggle to understand how Abraham could be willing to sacrifice Isaac, but rarely question how God could sacrifice Jesus for us? Why is that? Do we not think that Father experienced grief and horror at seeing Jesus suffer on the cross and then turn his back on him, something that Abraham never had to experience? Why is Abraham's decision disturbing, but Father's is not? Have we somehow discounted the pain that Father and Jesus experienced by sacrificing to demonstrate their love for us?

John went on to describe that God did not send Jesus into the world to judge the world, but to save the world (John 3:17). So, Jesus' presence in the world was due to the fact that Father sent him here. Abraham sent Ishmael into the wilderness; Father sent Jesus from heaven into the wilderness of the world. The word for "to send" is the verb form of apostle, which means "sent one." Jesus reiterated this when he declared to his disciples that, just as the Father had sent (apostollo) him into the world, so also he sent (pimpo) them into the world. Curiously, Jesus used a different word in reference to his disciples. The word used of Jesus is to send, as on a mission, while the word used for the disciples tends to carry the meaning of dispatch. Jesus had a different sending than ours. Jesus was sent into the world to lay down his life to save the world. We are not called to save the world, but dispatched into the world to declare what Jesus has done for the world. Jesus is not of the world, but from heaven. We are of the earth and adopted into heaven through Jesus, so we are not sent from heaven to earth; we are dispatched into all the earth (John 20:21).

However, what does it mean that God so loved the world that he gave his son? Like he asked of Abraham, God sacrificed his son, Jesus. So, when we make the statement that there can be no greater love than that which exists between the Father and the Son, there does seem to be one greater love. The Father, by sacrificing Jesus, demonstrates a greater love for us than he even had for

Jesus—just as Jesus demonstrated a greater love for us than he did for his own life. I don't know about you, but I struggle to grasp the significance of what Jesus and Father did for us on the cross. I also understand that it doesn't fit with human understanding, but we should never let our lack of understanding hinder us from grasping the magnitude of truth and Father's love for us. I had never considered Jesus' death in that light, and I find it extraordinary and humbling—how do you feel about it?

The more I grasp that truth, the more it has to change my life. John 3:16 means that you and I, as part of the world, possess Father God's greatest love and affection. In other words, there is nothing more for God to do to demonstrate his love for us. What significance does that have upon our life? If Father gave Jesus for us, then will he not also fulfill every prophetic promise made to us? Will he not give us everything we need to live and expand the kingdom on earth? While he may not immediately heal our diseases, will he not give grace to pursue him regardless? If Father gave Jesus for us, then he is willing to give us anything and everything else, because there is nothing greater for God to give than Jesus. Our lives must be transformed. Fear and anxiety should not ever co-exist with that type of love.

Much of Christianity uses fear to encourage people to follow Jesus. However, Father uses love. Fear motivates us to obey out of duty and obligation. There is not much joy or peace in that type of Christianity. There is only joy and peace when we obey Father out of love, the same type of love that he displayed for us when he gave Jesus so that, in Jesus, we might not perish but enjoy eternal life.

Questions for Reflection

1. What are the competing loves in your life? Who are the Isaacs in your life? Wrap them up, and lay them at the cross so that you might receive an even greater gift back from Jesus.
2. How does Abraham's willingness to sacrifice Isaac impact the way that you understand Father's love for you?
3. How is fear and anxiety unnecessary after you discover the magnitude of Father's love for you?

FOURTEEN

Jesus Defeats Despair

IN THE LAST CHAPTER, we saw God's unfathomable love for us, demonstrated in the sacrifice of Jesus on the cross. Jesus loved us more than his own life, so he laid it down to redeem us. Father loved us more than Jesus' life, so he sacrificed Jesus on the cross to bring us back into relationship with him. This chapter will explore these themes further. Why would God do such a thing? What is it about us that God loves so much?

Before we do so, I want to set the stage a bit. Several years ago, many disturbing events took place in just a matter of weeks. I want to touch on three, one personal, one local and one national. In August of 2014, I officiated the memorial service of a young man who had taken his own life—the son of good friends of ours. He was also a very good friend of our daughter and sons. What was especially troubling to me about his death was that he was a gifted and thoughtful young man. He had attended Christian schools his entire life. He led worship teams in school and was part of worship teams at our church. I find it deeply troubling when followers of Jesus take their lives. Then, we got the news that a young mother from a local community was missing. Several days later, her body was found in a nearby town. She too, had taken her life. She was a wife and mother of two young children. I find it troubling that a young woman and mother, who has so much to live for, took her life. Then just a bit later, we learned that a famous actor and comedian took his own life. Again, here was a man who was at the top of his field —famous and wealthy—yet he took his life. Is that not troubling?

As followers of Jesus, such troubling events take us back to how Jesus told us to live, and they remind us to compare his picture of life with how we are presently living. It raises a question for me, which I pose to you now. For what are we living? I follow that with a second question. Is what you are living for eternal? I ask those questions, because several weeks ago, I came across some words of Jesus that struck me in a completely different way than I had previously considered.

At times, Jesus said some things that were hard to digest. Sometimes he even appeared harsh and unyielding. His words in Luke 14:25-35 are strong and harsh. He tells us we must hate our loved ones. He tells us we must hate our own life. He tells us we must bear our own cross. He tells us we must give up all of our possessions. We are to count the cost of following Jesus and the cost of following the world. Jesus tells us that the Christian life is one where we will often feel excluded. We are to be one hundred percent devoted to Jesus. Jesus' disciples were.

They left family and the livelihood of businesses in order to follow Jesus. They didn't work all week and follow Jesus in their spare time; Jesus was their life, 24/7. With Jesus, they were mocked and ridiculed by the mainstream community. The question remains—why is Jesus so harsh and demanding here? What is his point? What is his motivation? Jesus indicated that his followers will live a fundamentally different life from those who follow the world.

I have to wonder if many of us have subtly bought into a lie. That lie says, basically, ask Jesus for forgiveness, then work hard, get an education, get married, have children, go to church, and you will be happy. However, that lifestyle does not seem to be working for many people. What I find equally disturbing is that the only answer contemporary Christianity seems to have for that inner dissatisfaction is to work harder and do more—pray more, read the Bible more, attend church more, and get more involved. For some, those suggestions produce more fatigue and can lack fulfillment. For those individuals, Christianity, as it has come to be known in the west, isn't working very well.

Many people are very adept at keeping themselves so busy that they don't seem to notice that what they are living for will not last. Their busy-ness blinds them. Over the years, I have had opportunity to speak with some people who have told me that they would much rather be doing something else that they felt was more significant, but didn't pay as well. Some take the risk, slow down enough, and realize that much of what our culture teaches is empty and meaningless, very similar to how Solomon described all the good things to which he saw people giving their lives. Because Solomon's words in Ecclesiastes are so disturbing, some Christians teach that they were the words of a misguided king. Rather, I think Solomon was right on the mark, and Jesus warned us of not heeding his words in Luke 14.

So, let me return to Luke 14. It seems to me that Jesus is speaking very bluntly with us. Every decision that we make has a cost. Jesus tells us to count it. If we are going to follow Jesus, there is a price to pay. We voluntarily lay down our daily lives to live for Jesus, not the world. Paul called this a living sacrifice. Following Jesus will cost us something. Abraham was willing to sacrifice Isaac. Moses faced his fear and returned to Egypt. David had to run for his life for a time. The disciples left homes and jobs. Paul sacrificed his freedom to return to Jerusalem and go to Rome. However, in the above cases, each individual considered what God gave them far superior to what they had given up. We receive joy by being in relationship with Jesus and having a life that will have eternal significance.

This leads us to another question. How are we to live? Are we to renounce marriage, family, and work? No, we are called to live in the world. When Paul gave instruction to the Corinthians about marriage, I believe he was explaining what Jesus meant here. Jesus did not condemn work, marriage or family, all of which were created by Father, but he placed them in eternal perspective. Nothing on the earth is to be your destiny or purpose, because they are passing away. We are to live for the eternal. So, our purpose on earth must be eternal, not temporal (1 Corinthians 7:25-35). Paul encouraged the

Corinthians to remain single so that they would not be distracted from following Jesus. His reason was that anyone who was married needed to dedicate time and energy to a spouse and possibly children. While marriage and children are a blessing, they can also be a distraction from Jesus. Paul teaches us that when we marry, we must keep our focus on Jesus. That is what Paul meant by being married, but living as though we are not.

In other words, your life's purpose is not to become wealthy or famous. Your life's purpose is not to be successful in your career. Your life's purpose is an assignment from heaven that will leave eternal results. It might be building or working in a business. It might be giving comfort to the sick and dying. It might be raising children. It might be giving your life to worship and prayer. In any case, it is refusing to allow the blessings of the world to distract you from your eternal purpose, which is centered upon undivided devotion to Jesus. Paul and Jesus help us grasp that kingdom concept.

This leads us to another question: Why are Jesus' and Paul's teachings so important? There is a direct connection between how much we love the world and our intimacy with Jesus and Father. The more we are distracted by the blessings of the world, the further relationally we will be from Jesus and Father. The more that we live in the world but refuse to be distracted by it, the freer we are to be close to Jesus and Father.

Intimacy with God (Father, Jesus, and Holy Spirit) leads to a discussion of who we are and an examination of why Father loves us so much. I believe that many of us misunderstand Father, his love, and his glory. Let me explain. Here is what I have been taught, or at least what I understood to have been taught. God is the greatest, and he must be loved above all others. Therefore, God loves himself above all others. God's glory is the greatest and most magnificent; therefore, we are to seek God's glory. Therefore, God himself seeks his own glory.

What is odd about those two concepts—God loving himself more than all else and seeking his own glory above all else—is that I cannot find either conclusion taught in Scripture. I can find nowhere in Scripture where it says God loves himself above all else. Rather, I do find that God loves humankind so much that he sacrificed Jesus (John 3:16). I do find that we are to love God above everything else (Matthew 22:37-39). Scripture says that we know how to love because God first loved us (1 John 4:19). Here is the problem with what is often taught about God's self-love and self-glorification. How can we learn to love God and others from a God who loves himself more than anything else? Would that not teach us to love ourselves? How do parents teach their children to love? They teach their children to love, not by loving themselves, but by sacrificially loving their children, which the Bible teaches that God does for us.

Jesus said that there is no greater love than for someone to lay down their life for their friends (John 15:13). Jesus proved that when he died on the cross. John described Father's great love for us when he gave Jesus to die (John 3:16). That is earthshaking. God is not a celestial egotist, trying to convince the world that he is the greatest and, therefore, we must love him. Rather, he has done and is doing everything to demonstrate that he loves us in the same way that we are to love him back. Father's and Jesus' love for us is the rationale for us to live exactly how Jesus told us to live in Luke 14 and exactly how Paul describes in 1 Corinthians 7.

I think what Jesus was doing in Luke 14 was saving us from a life that is beneath our calling. However, if we ignore Jesus' words, we run the risk of disappointment, perhaps depression, and even despair.

Sometimes, we think God only loves us because we were in such need. Scripture says that we were dead in our trespasses and sins when Jesus died for us (Ephesians 2:1-8). In the Old Testament, we are described as an abandoned infant girl about to die due to exposure, but we were rescued by God's grace and compassion (Ezekiel 16:1-7). From these passages, we can get this view of God's love for us because we were so pitiful. While this view has biblical foundation, it is an incomplete view of God's love for us. We can summarize that incomplete view by saying that God has to love us because we are his creation. He is compassionate, and I am so needy that he has to love me. But, while God's love is compassionate, and we are needy, his love for us is much greater. To understand, we must understand who God created us to be. A look at God's glory helps us grasp a greater understanding.

Although God's glory is not explicitly mentioned in Genesis 1 and 2, who we were created to be is. Scripture clearly states that every man and woman is created in the image of God. That means that everywhere we go, we reflect the image of God. As the image bearers on earth, God gave us the authority to rule the earth. This authority was lost when Adam led us into sin, but was restored when Jesus defeated sin and death on the cross and through his resurrection. However, Scripture continues to reveal that we are actually more than image-bearers of God. There are almost four hundred references to "glory" in the Bible; it might surprise you to learn that many of those references liken us to God's glory.

We were created with a purpose and a destiny to rule, crowned with God's glory (Psalm 8:5-8; Isaiah 60:2-3; 62:2-3). A ruler's crown sets him or her apart from all others. It is a symbol of authority. God's glory is our crown and authority to rule over all of creation. David said that all things have been placed under man's feet. Jesus expanded our authority to all authority in heaven and on earth which has been given to him and now delegated to us (Matthew 28:18). Isaiah noted that this glory with which we are crowned will one day draw all nations as sons and daughters of God (Isaiah 60:2-3).

Along with glory, we will receive a new name, given to us from our Father. I believe this is our family name received directly from Father; but also, just as parents name their children, so does our heavenly Father name us and declare our identity. As in the Old Testament, names were a prophetic declaration of a child's destiny, so also our identifying name received from our Father declares who we are. We have much to look forward to (Isaiah 62:2-3).

Isaiah revealed much about the glory of God. In Isaiah 42:8, he wrote something that I believe has caused confusion, because it has been misunderstood. In this passage, we read God saying that he would not give his glory to another, nor his praise to graven images or idols. This is one of the passages that has caused some to conclude that God seeks his glory above all else and that he loves himself above all others. However, Isaiah 42:8 is in the context of allowing false gods to share and possess God's glory. Idols are created by people, not by God. What is true of an idol is not necessarily true of us. Of course, God would not share his glory with false gods, but this does not mean that God seeks his own glory above all else. We will see this more clearly in other passages.

Scripture reveals that glory is more than a characteristic. Ezekiel received a unique revelation regarding this. Often, we think of God's glory as something, rather than someone. However, Ezekiel saw that the glory of God was standing before him (Ezekiel 3:23). This was new revelation. Glory was personified. Ezekiel recognized the glory standing there, because he had seen him before. In Ezekiel 1:26-28, Ezekiel described what he saw earlier and what he saw again in Ezekiel 3. He saw a being on a throne that seemed to be composed of fire, whose radiance he called the glory of God. The similarity of what John saw in Revelation 1:12-18 causes me to think that Jesus is this same glory of God, housed in human flesh and brought to earth. What does this mean? The glory of God is a person, who became a man and dwelt among us (John 1:14). When we read John 1:14 in light of Ezekiel 3:23, we see that God's glory is not merely what Jesus had. Glory is who Jesus was and is. Glory is Jesus' identity, revealed to John.

Ezekiel, along with other prophets during and after the Babylonian exile, revealed a new revelation. Early prophets like David revealed that God's glory was always seen in the heavens, but these latter prophets announced that God's glory dwelt on earth. Ezekiel saw God standing on earth, before him. Habakkuk saw God's glory filling the earth (Habakkuk 2:14). Notice Habakkuk revealed that not only would the earth be filled with the glory of God, but also the knowledge of God's glory. The word "knowledge" is not merely an intellectual knowledge, but it is relational and experiential knowledge. Zechariah moved even further, because he attached God's glory with his people. To highlight his glory, God went after his people who were dispersed in the nations, for they were the apple of his eye (Zechariah 2:8). Zechariah connected God's glory with his people and with the great affection that Father feels for all of his people. The latter prophets revealed two things. They personified God's glory, and they revealed that the glory came to earth and filled it. Sound like someone we know?

Jesus made a statement that should cause us to pause and reflect. It is not unusual for the concept to be taught that God seeks his own glory. This comes from the fact that God's glory is the highest, so it would be natural for him to seek the highest glory. While this statement is logical, it is not necessarily biblical. Jesus stated that he did not seek his own glory (John 8:50). It would seem strange for Jesus, being God and the highest revelation of the Father, to declare that he did not seek his own glory, and then claim that the Father does seek his own glory. While Scripture says that the Father does not share his glory with idols, this does not necessarily mean that he seeks his own glory. Rather, it is more consistent to understand that Jesus was revealing the Father when he declared that he did not seek his own glory, and neither does the Father.

Paul spoke of a future glory that will be revealed in us. That glory causes the present difficulties to pale in significance (Romans 8:18). Paul went on to reveal that God's people were prepared for glory (Romans 9:23). To his people, God gave wisdom, which bore fruit in his people's own glory (1 Corinthians 2:7). In teaching the Corinthians on the relationships between husbands and wives, Paul revealed something about glory. He declared that man was the glory of God. Ezekiel had seen a personification of God's glory, and now Paul declared that men personified God's glory. This does not mean that women are not a personification of God's glory, because this was not Paul's point. He was instructing the Corinthians that men and women were to relate to one another in appropriate ways. Since men were the glory of God, then women, being created from man, would also be a personification of God's glory, as well as man's (1 Corinthians 11:7).

The idea that man is God's glory is revealed to be even more significant by what Paul wrote later. He described different types of glory: heavenly and earthly, the sun, moon, and stars, etc. However, men are specifically the glory of God (1 Corinthians 15:40). Paul went on to declare that the glory that was revealed in the Old Testament was surpassed with the coming of Jesus and continues to increase. As we grow in Jesus, we are transformed into even more divine glory. The expression, "glory to glory," does not refer to things we do, things we experience, or places we go, but to who we are! This was Paul's point when he used the expression, "glory to glory," in 2 Corinthians 3:18. We are being transformed into the same image of Jesus, progressing from one glory to another higher glory.

Paul's discussion of glory in 1 & 2 Corinthians sheds light on his instruction in Romans 3. In Romans 3:23,

Paul wrote that all men have fallen short of God's glory. I have always taken that verse to reveal a lack of performance. Men do not live up to God's standard of perfection. However, if Paul wrote about men being the glory of God, then perhaps falling short of glory is not about performance, but rather living below who we truly are. We do this because we do not really understand who we are; if we did, perhaps we would not fall short of the glory given to us.

Scripture gives us one reason that God loves us so much. We are his glory. We are his pride and joy, not based on what we do, but because of who we are. As an example, young men are interesting to observe. Often, young men are not at all interested in holding an infant. If they do, they also often appear uncomfortable and awkward. That all changes when that infant is his own son. Now, that small child who communicates primarily by screaming and wakes his parents up at all hours of the night—causing them to exist in a constant state of fatigue for months—is revealed to all friends and family with great pride and joy. The infant does absolutely nothing, except that he or she is a son or daughter, the glory of his or her parents. When we grasp the amazing concept that we are God's glory on earth, it changes the way we live. Jesus' revelation of being God's glory and transferring his glory to us defeats all need for despair in this life.

Questions for Reflection

1. When Jesus tells us to "hate" our closest

relatives, our life, and our possessions, what do you think he desires to produce in our life?
2. How do we live out the revelation of loving Jesus above all else?
3. How can the revelation that we are God's glory transform someone's life?

FIFTEEN

Prophetic Crossroads Determine Our Future

SEVERAL YEARS AGO, I read Bill Johnson's book, "Strengthening Yourself in the Lord." He took those words from 1 Samuel 30:6, when David strengthened himself in the Lord. The text does not say how David strengthened himself; Bill Johnson does not either. However, I believe that another passage sheds light on what happened to David at that low point of his life. We read a very similar phrase when Jonathan declared prophetically regarding David's and his own future in 1 Samuel 23:15-19. Recently, I have pondered Jonathan's words, because he rightly declared that David would be king, but mistakenly declared that he would serve David as king. Questions arose as I pondered Jonathan's words; did he get it wrong? That is what I originally thought; then recently, I received a very different insight.

Before we look at that question regarding Jonathan, let's take a broader look at prophecy. God gives us prophetic words to give us a glimpse of what will happen if we do not change or what could happen if we do. The Bible is filled with examples of this.

Lot warned the men engaged to marry his daughters that Sodom was about to be destroyed, but they refused to act and were destroyed with the rest of the city (Genesis 19:12-14). Scripture says that Lot appeared to be jesting. These two young men failed to acknowledge Lot's words and perished as a result. They didn't have to perish; they could have been saved, but their unbelief prevented their salvation.

Daniel 4 is a fascinating chapter. Often, we do not realize that Daniel did not author this chapter—Nebuchadnezzar did. In Daniel 4, Nebuchadnezzar had a dream of a majestic tree cut down and chained for seven periods of time. When he interpreted the dream, Daniel warned the king that he was about to be judged. Daniel urged Nebuchadnezzar to repent so that what had been revealed would not happen. In other words, Daniel indicated that Nebuchadnezzar's response could influence the outcome of the prophetic dream. Nebuchadnezzar failed to repent, so he was judged and lost his mind for a period of time. Nebuchadnezzar's failure to believe caused him to live out the prophetic warning.

Jonah declared to the Ninevites that they would be judged after forty days. However, they heeded Jonah's words and repented. Jonah's prophetic word did not take place, because the Ninevites acted according to the word and repented. Jonah's prophecy was not false because it was not fulfilled. It was not fulfilled because the Ninevites repented. The Ninevites reveal that prophetic words are not necessarily a concrete declaration of the future. The appropriate action can either change a prophetic warning or bring about a prophetic promise.

We need to ask the question, why does God give us prophetic words in the first place? I believe they are an example of his grace and mercy. Why did God send Jonah? Was it because he wanted the Ninevites to know he would punish them? Or, was it so that he could show them mercy after they repented? God's explanation to Jonah indicates the latter. God warned them so that they would not be judged and destroyed. It was his mercy that sent Jonah.

We also know that prophetic words are given to encourage us. The fact that they are given to encourage indicates that prophetic words are often given to us to choose and pursue a life path that may not be obvious to us according to wise counsel and circumstances. God gives us positive prophetic words to encourage us to contend for a reality that leads us into fulfilling the assignments he has laid out for us. He gives us prophetic words so that we would fulfill what Paul wrote to the Ephesians in Ephesians 2:10, "For we are God's workmanship, created in Christ Jesus to do good works, which God prepared beforehand, that we would walk in them." Ephesians 2:10 is an interesting verse to ponder in light of our purpose to know Father in Jesus and to complete our assignments, prepared in advance for us to do. The existence of prophetic words also indicates that we may face life circumstances that may encourage us to abandon a life direction that God wants us to pursue. If circumstances would lead us normally to pursue God's path for us, then the need for prophetic words would not be necessary. If the Ninevites would have repented on their own, God would not have needed to send the prophet. Prophetic words lead us to pursue some assignments that we might not naturally pursue. Consider the following.

An angel appeared to Gideon and told him he would deliver Israel from the Midianites. Gideon would have never come to that conclusion without the prophetic word given to him. He even needed the fleece test and the dream of a Midianite soldier to pursue God's prophetic word to him.

Neither Saul nor David were kingly material when Samuel anointed them, but Samuel's anointing and prophetic words to them led them to be kings over Israel. Saul had to be encouraged to take that step because he was afraid. David had to be encouraged to continue on that path because he feared for his life.

In Corinth, Paul needed a prophetic word from Jesus not to flee Corinth as he had fled Damascus, Jerusalem, Philippi, Thessalonica, and Berea. Prior to that prophetic word, Paul typically fled when persecution came. After the prophetic word, Paul never fled any city due to persecution. His life was dramatically changed by his encounter with Jesus in Corinth (Acts 18:9-11).

So, this leads us back to the original question. Why didn't Jonathan become David's right hand man? It would be easy to say that Jonathan just misunderstood and that he got part of it right and part of it wrong. That is a possibility, but I want to offer another possibility. The prophecy Jonathan gave for his own life never came to pass, because he did not make decisions according to that word. 1 Samuel 23:18 says that Jonathan and David made a covenant. David remained at Horesh, while Jonathan went to his house. Why did Jonathan return to his house, if his place was to serve at David's side? In the spiritual realm, David was already king of Israel. David became king of Israel from the moment Samuel anointed him when David was a boy. Samuel had anointed him, and both Jonathan and Saul had recognized it.

In biblical times, God chose the kings for his people. People did not. Therefore, David was king from the moment he was anointed. When the men of Judah recognized him as their king and then seven years later, the rest of Israel did as well, they only recognized a reality that had already existed for a long time. In the same way, Jesus has been king over all the earth since his resurrection, even though few men on earth recognize him as such.

So, why didn't Jonathan take his place with David? I don't know the answer to that question, but I believe Jonathan's decision to not act according to his prophetic word had significant consequences for them all.

I cannot biblically prove what I am about to say, but I believe it is a possibility that we should consider. Jonathan's decision to return home aligned him with his father, Saul, not with David. It kept him in his past worldly identity as heir to Israel's throne and not his prophetic identity with David. Saul was actively opposed to David, yet Jonathan remained aligned with his father. Fast forward into the future. When Saul went into his last battle against the Philistines, Jonathan was with Saul, not with David. In battle, Jonathan, Saul, and two of Jonathan's brothers perished.

What were the consequences of Jonathan's decision? Since Jonathan had not taken his place with David, Joab became the commander of David's army, not Jonathan. Joab was a violent man who would murder both Abner and Amasa without David's knowledge—doing so in order to preserve his position with David. If Jonathan had been there, Joab would never have risen to that position. After Saul's death, civil war broke out between Judah and Israel, because Abner made Saul's surviving son, Ishbosheth, king over Israel. That probably would not have happened after Saul's death if Jonathan had been still alive and with David. Israel, who loved Jonathan, probably would have followed Jonathan's example and supported David. Civil war between Judah and Israel might never have taken place.

Would it have been risky for Jonathan to leave everything to follow David when he had a comfortable home? Absolutely. Such a decision was unheard of. Jonathan may have lost everything to follow David, but I suggest that it was much more costly to not act upon the prophetic word he had declared. Jesus said that he who seeks to save his life will lose it. Jonathan unintentionally became an example of Jesus' words. Jonathan's decision to return home reflected that he still lived in the identity as the king's son and heir to Israel's throne, not as David's right hand man.

This is the point! We are given prophetic words so that we will make decisions that appear risky in the natural realm, but are life giving in the spiritual realm. It was and is unheard of for an heir to the throne to step aside and serve another as king. That is what Jonathan prophetically declared, but he failed to make life decisions according to that prophecy. It is interesting to consider that David may have had to spend a longer time in the wilderness, because God was graciously extending the window of opportunity for Jonathan to step into his prophetic destiny. Why do I say this? Read what Peter wrote in 2 Peter 3:3-10. Our Father is patient, and he extends the time to give opportunity for all people to come to repentance. I think this is more than praying the sinners' prayer, but pursuing the prophetic declarations made to us. Consider what Jesus said at the end of his parable about the persistent widow (Luke 18:8). When Jesus returns, will he find us pursuing our prophetic dreams, or will he find us at home, like Jonathan, trying to preserve an identity that no longer exists?

When David was in the wilderness, Jonathan was not the only one who prophesied that he would be king. Even more clearly than Jonathan, we know that Saul was a prophet. When Saul became king, God gave him a spirit of prophesy which surprised the people who knew him (1 Samuel 10:5-13). Saul was the other prophet who declared David would be king (1 Samuel 24). However, like Jonathan, Saul failed to act upon his own prophetic word. Like Jonathan, we read that he returned home and continued to live an identity that prophetically was no longer his.

Some prophetic words are given, but they are dependent upon a right response on our part, otherwise they are no longer possible. Reflect on the nation of Israel's response to the spies' report. Fear caused the ten spies to discourage the people; faith led Caleb and Joshua to encourage the people to follow the prophetic promise to enter into the land. The people's decision to believe the appearance of the Canaanites' strength, and not the prophetic word, led to the ten spies dying by a plague. It almost resulted in all of Israel perishing, were it not for Moses and Aaron's prayer for them. It led Israel to attempt to make the prophetic word come true in their own strength, but resulted in their defeat by the Canaanites and Amalekites. Finally, it led to their remaining in the desert for forty years while the next generation prepared to enter into the Promised Land. Even though they failed in this instance, they still had a future and a purpose. They were to prepare a new generation.

I believe that Saul would have had a future had he stepped aside and allowed David to rule as king. Before, when Samuel had declared that the kingdom was removed from Saul, we read nowhere that Saul had to die first. However, it is probable that Saul could not imagine his life not being king, so the only option was for him to die. Tragically, Jonathan died with him. I don't believe it had to be that way.

Why do I say that he had a future after stepping aside from being king? First of all, God is merciful and desires all men to come to repentance, like we have already seen. Many years later, there was another man named Saul, who persecuted the Lord's anointed. King Saul persecuted David. Saul of Tarsus persecuted Jesus. Both were confronted with the anointed one's mercy. David showed mercy to Saul and confronted him. But, Saul did not act upon that revelation. He continued to kick against the goads. However, when confronted by Jesus, Saul of Tarsus did repent and was transformed into a different man who served his new king rather than trying to destroy him. I believe Saul of Tarsus is a picture of what might have been if King Saul had repented, because our Father is merciful.

God's mercy causes us to consider something else about Saul. We often think of God taking the kingdom away from Saul as punishment and judgment, but have you ever considered the possibility that it was God's mercy? Saul had demonstrated that he was not up to being Israel's king. God knew that if Saul remained in that position, it would destroy him. In fact, it did. Saul first lost his mind and eventually his life.

Sometimes we miss a prophetic window; it is not the end of the world if we acknowledge that we missed it and ask the next logical question—what next? This is a superior decision to sinking into despair and living as though we have no more hope. That decision will lead to death; we need to pursue the next prophetic destiny Father reveals to us.

You may be at a prophetic crossroads in your life. You may be trying to hold onto something past, like Saul. It may be time to step into a new and yet unknown future that Father has for you. On the other hand, you may have received a glimpse of what Father has for you. It may be time for you to start living according to that glimpse and stop living according an old identity.

Questions for Reflection

1. What might it cost you to pursue a new path for your life?
2. If you don't pursue a God-given path, what outcomes might take place in your life?
3. Who are those individuals in your life who will encourage you to take risks in order to pursue what Father is revealing to you?

SIXTEEN

How Are We to Understand the Fear of the Lord?

AWHILE BACK, I was struck with an apparent contradiction that comes up among Christians. An apparent contradiction is not a real contradiction, but at times, it feels like one. Often, such contradictions come from our understanding of words and the meanings that they take on in certain situations. For example, consider the word "little." We all know what the word "little" means; it describes a person, or an object, or a concept as being small. It can refer to either size or quantity. Nothing earthshaking there; it is a rather straight forward word. Yet, consider this situation and the meaning of the word "little." You go over to a friend's house and are invited in. They have just finished dinner and say to you, "there is a little cake left, would you like some?" What does "little" mean? It takes on the meaning that there is enough for you to have a piece of cake. Very straight forward, we get the meaning. Now, consider this statement. You come home, and as soon as you enter the door, a family member says this, "Hey, we've only got a little milk in the fridge, could you go to the store and get some?" What is the meaning of "little" in this statement? There is not enough milk, and again, the meaning is clear and straightforward. However, the meaning of "little" in the first sentence is the direct opposite of the second. In the first, the word "little" means that there is enough for you to have cake, but in the second, it means that there is not enough, so you have to go to the store and get some more. Same word, two opposite meanings.

Most of the time, we don't give a second thought and would never consider those statements to have a contradictory meaning of the word "little." Yet, sometimes when we consider passages in the Bible, we forget that words can often take on very different meanings. In those times, we get confused about what the word or verse means.

The Bible teaches that we are to live in freedom without fear. Paul wrote that it is for freedom that Jesus set us free (Galatians 5:1). Furthermore, Jesus often rebuked his disciples for being afraid. That sounds very straightforward and often times it is, but consider this question: Are we to fear God? Although we make a great effort to teach living without fear, to be accurate, we must affirm that, yes, the Bible does teach that we are to fear God. Let's look at a few passages.

In the midst of Job's discourse on acquiring wisdom, he explained that you cannot purchase wisdom, but that it is only acquired through the fear of the Lord (Job 28:28). We would all agree that wisdom is a good thing, so in this case, fearing the Lord God is very good, because in so doing, we acquire the wisdom needed to live. David went even further than Job. David affirmed that God blesses those who fear him—specifically providing them meat or prey (Psalm 111:5). All of us desire provision and blessings in our life; David says that the way to receive such blessing is through fearing God. Again, fearing God is shown to be a very good thing. Like both Job and David, Solomon affirmed the goodness of fearing God and its connection to wisdom (Proverbs 9:7-12). Solomon declared that the fear of the Lord is the beginning of wisdom (Proverbs 9:10). These three men clearly indicate that the foundation of a good life is fearing God.

In the New Testament, Jesus also affirmed the wisdom and goodness of fearing God. However, with Jesus, we begin to understand that there is a good fear and a bad fear (Matthew 10:24-28). Jesus warned his disciples about fearing man, while at the same time instructing them to fear God (Matthew 10:24-28). Jesus declared that his followers were not to fear humans, who can only harm the body, but to fear God who can bring destruction to both body and soul. Peter reiterated what was taught in the Old Testament. He declared to Cornelius and his entire household that no matter what nation a person is from, God will bless those who fear him (Acts 10:34-35). In Hebrews, we see a connection between fearing God and entering the rest that we enjoy in the kingdom. While our fear of the Lord leads us to enjoy rest found in the kingdom, it is implied that failure to fear the Lord may jeopardize entry into kingdom rest (Hebrews 4:1).

Clearly as lovers of Jesus, we are commanded to fear God. We are promised provision and rest when we do. So, fearing God is a good thing, right? The obvious answer is "yes." Well, this is where the apparent contradiction enters. If we are to fear God, then why did Jesus use the very same word when he so often commanded his followers not to be afraid?

Consider, once again, the parable of the talents found in Matthew 25:14-30. Jesus described three servants, each of whom were given talents according to each's ability. The master, representing God, gave them the talents. The first received five talents and earned five more. The second received two talents and earned two more. However, it is on the third servant that I want to focus. He received one talent, but he buried his. Why he buried it is the key question. He tells us why he buried it. He was afraid; in other words, he feared his master. Now according to all that we've seen so far, this servant should be blessed, because he feared his master who, in the parable, represents the Lord God. However, the master curses this servant and calls him wicked and lazy. How can it be that we are commanded to fear God, and yet, when this man fears God, he is condemned? We cannot get around this dilemma by saying there must be two different words, because the exact same word is used in this parable and when Jesus tells us to fear God and not fear men. In one situation, a person fears God and is blessed, and in another, a person fears God and is condemned. How can this be? We need to look closer at why the man was afraid of the master/God.

The servant tells us why he was afraid. He believed his master/God to be a hard man and implied that he was even a thief, because he reaped where he had not sown. In other words, this servant believed a lie about God. His fear was the product of mistrust and not love for God. He believed God to be harsh and unjust. This lie has been rooted in humans since the Garden of Eden. It is a lie that

Jesus addressed directly. He taught that God is a loving Father who cares for his children and will take care of them, while the world is a place that will be the source of tribulation for those who love God. The lie that the third servant believed is a deeply rooted lie in many Christians.

Consider how many people believe that God will make them do something they do not want to do. They may believe he will make them do a job they despise or live in a place they cannot stand. This subtle mistrust of God is rooted in a lie that works its way into our thinking. For example, I have heard some say they don't want to be a missionary because God will send them to some horrible place to serve.

We may even develop a schizophrenic view of God, similar to a "good cop, bad cop" understanding. We mistrust God the Father, because we think he exists to punish us and keep us in line—and we think He will make us do what we don't want to do. However, we develop love and trust for Jesus, because he is our Savior and will forgive us. After all, sometimes, we even misunderstand passages like Hebrews 7:23-25. We read about ideas like Jesus living to make intercession before the Father—and conclude that if Jesus didn't make intercession for us, God the Father would strike us with lightning because we do not reach his level of perfection. Nowhere in Hebrews 7 should we conclude that God is angry with us and desires to destroy us. Rather, we should view Jesus' intercession as a means of releasing Father's love, blessing, and provision for us, because as Father loves Jesus, so also he loves us. The lie is that we need to be continually saved from God's wrath, when the truth is that Father loves to bless us and wants us to be set free.

The response of the third servant helps us understand that, while there is a healthy fear of God which brings blessing and resembles "honor" and "reverence," there is also an unhealthy fear of God that resembles "terror." The terror of God, which is inappropriate, explains why Jesus so often told his disciples not to be afraid, while at the same time instructing them to fear God.

Have you ever considered how often Jesus instructs us not to be afraid? Remember, after Jesus fed the five thousand, he sent his disciples in a boat to cross the Sea of Galilee, while he went up on a hill to pray. In the middle of the night, he crossed the lake by walking on the water. When the disciples saw him, they freaked out. Do you remember what Jesus said to them? He said, "take courage, it is I; do not be afraid" (Matthew 14:25-27). Jesus commanded his disciples not to be afraid in his presence. Why did Jesus tell them this? It is inappropriate, as children of Father, for us to be terror stricken in Jesus' presence.

When Peter, James, and John were on the mountain with Jesus, they seemed to be perfectly fine watching Jesus converse with Moses and Elijah, but as soon as the voice from the cloud said, "this is my beloved son in whom I'm well pleased," the disciples shook with fear. What did Jesus tell them? He told them to get up and not be afraid (Matthew 17:3-7). Again, Jesus commanded them to stop being afraid in Father's presence. Not only is it inappropriate for us to be afraid in Jesus' presence, it is also inappropriate for us to be afraid in Father's presence.

The apostle John, who was present on both of the occasions when Jesus commanded his disciples not to be afraid, explained why it is inappropriate for us to be afraid of God. John made a profound connection in 1 John 4:15-19 when he declared that God is love and perfect love drives out fear. With these words, John connected fear and love. John is not overturning the truth that fear of God is the beginning of wisdom, but he is using the word "fear" in a different sense—just as we've seen earlier. Just as the word "little" can mean different things depending on the context, so also can the word "fear." The type of fear that John refers to here is the type of fear that is equated with terror. This type of fear wars against love. This type of fear comes from condemnation, which has been removed in Jesus. Paul revealed to us that in Jesus, there is now no condemnation (Romans 8:1-2). In Jesus, we have been set free from condemnation. Love has cast out fear, and where there was once fear confidence now resides. We are to be confident in Jesus and Father's presence, which means it is inappropriate that we shrink back in fear.

John explains that the one who still exhibits this type of fear in God's presence reveals that he has not understood the magnitude of Father's love for us. This is why it is inconsistent for us to say that we can relate to Jesus and the Spirit but struggle to relate to the Father. Why? Jesus came to reveal the Father to us; this was his purpose. What we see and love in Jesus is the Father. Jesus told us that he would send the Holy Spirit as comforter who would come alongside us and lead us into all truth (John 16:13). If we are believing a lie, which results in fear of God's presence, John indicates that we need the Holy Spirit to guide us into the truth regarding who the Father is.

So how can we tell the difference between an appropriate fear of God, which leads to wisdom and blessing, and an inappropriate fear? We look at the fruit. An appropriate fear of God can be described as honor which produces confidence in the way that we live our life. On the other hand, inappropriate fear produces anxiety that leads to timidity, shame, and hiding in God's presence. Paul addressed this concept in his final letter to Timothy (2 Timothy 1:7) when he said that Father did not give us a Spirit of timidity but one of power, love and discipline.

As the word "fear" can be understood in multiple senses, so can the word "love." As appropriate fear can be distorted by lies we believe about God, so also can love be distorted. In 1 John 2:15-17, John addressed inappropriate love for the world that wars with love for God. It is clear that we are to love the world, because God loves the world (John 3:16). However, John is using the word "love" in a different sense in 1 John than he had earlier in his gospel. In the gospel of John, John used the word "love" in the sense of expressing love through giving for the good of another. However, in 1 John, he used the exact same word for an intense desire that is synonymous with lust. We are not to desire the things of this world— in other words, all those things that the world says you need to be happy. Even though many things in the world are good—even blessings from Father—they are and always will remain temporary. John declared that the world is passing away. Therefore, we are to resist the lie which tells us we need these blessings to be happy. Nevertheless, we are to still care about what happens to the world, seek the blessing of the world, and desire to see the kingdom expanded within the world. While the world is passing away, we are eternal. Although our physical bodies may deteriorate and even die, we are not passing away, for Solomon declared to us that God has placed eternity into our hearts (Ecclesiastes 3:11).

Questions for Reflection

1. How would you explain appropriate fear of the Lord?
2. Why do you think Jesus' disciples exhibited fear when they encountered Jesus' power?
3. In what ways can you apply Father's love for you to overcome inappropriate fear in your life?

SEVENTEEN

Conclusions

AFTER ALL THIS, how are we to live? What really has meaning in this life? At the end of Ecclesiastes, Solomon gives us insight. He reminds us to remember our Creator in the days of our youth and before the struggles of life come (Ecclesiastes 12:1). In this simple sentence, Solomon encourages us to lay a foundation of remembering our Father, because troubles in life do come. The remembrance serves as our foundation and strength to endure and find joy when difficult days enter our existence. Solomon concluded his treatise by reminding us to fear God and keep his commandments. How do we do this?

We must remember who we are and live according to our identity. In the movie "The Lion King," Simba, the young lion prince, forgot who he was after the death of his father. He ran, hid, and lived a life of "no worries," forgetting the responsibility of who he was, a prince—the rightful king. Jesus revealed to his followers that by entering into a relationship with him and following him, they had become children of the living God. The apostle Peter revealed that a child of God experiences a change in his or her very nature; the person becomes a partaker of the divine nature, sharing it with their heavenly Father, Holy Spirit, and Jesus. Jesus taught that the meek, in other words, his followers, will inherit the earth and consequently the kingdom of heaven. While Solomon told us to remember our Creator, Jesus taught us to remember our Father and that we are his children. Therefore, we cannot run and hide, but we have the responsibility to make a difference in the world, not through position, power or fame, but through all that the Holy Spirit is—love, joy, peace, patience, kindness, goodness, faithfulness, gentleness, and self-control.

While we are encouraged by Scripture to seek wisdom, the wise student recognizes that the increase of wisdom and knowledge increases both responsibility and grief. In the garden, God warned Adam and Eve about eating from the tree of the knowledge of good and evil. Their ignoring of his command plunged humanity into suffering and death. Relational knowledge of God and others draws us into wonderful relationships, but it also opens us up to experiencing that individual's grief. Knowledge of the world and its occurrences also leads us to the grief of suffering in people's lives. The only solution is to follow Jesus' way of living by continually pursuing an intimate relationship with Father, who gives us his strength and wisdom to respond to the griefs and pain we encounter in the world.

In affluent societies, there are many opportunities to enjoy entertainment and pursue hobbies. While there is nothing wrong with pursuing hobbies or enjoying recreation, Solomon reminds us that they cannot give us lasting fulfillment. They are enjoyable for the moment, but they are not to replace our relationship with Jesus, which provides comfort in times of difficulty. Jesus told the weary to come to him; he did not teach his followers to find comfort in an endless array of entertainment options.

The affluence of many modern societies relates to another of Solomon's topics—wealth. While money is a necessary part of our life, the love of it causes great problems for people. Furthermore, it does not do for us what we think it will: make us happy. We work hard to earn more money; motivating us is a subtle lie that having a certain level of money will lead to happiness. Unfortunately, this is not true. All we need to do is observe those who currently have the level of wealth we think we need. As we do, we discover that those individuals are not as happy as we assume we would be if we had their wealth. Jesus pointed out that the secret to contentment is in relationship with our heavenly Father. We have been created in the image of God. Therefore, things that pass away cannot satisfy us; only that which is eternal can bring true contentment. It is the pursuit of an ever-increasing relationship with God our Father that leads us to joy and contentment.

If affluence, education, or success will not bring us fulfillment, then what will? Jesus shows us. It is in our relationship with Jesus that we find fulfillment. Paul reminded us that it is the pursuit of knowing Jesus that gives meaning to life, not the accomplishments that attract the world. Jesus reminded his disciples that it is not success that brings life, but knowledge of him. The reason is simple. Everything on earth will be lost; Jesus said heaven and earth will pass away, but his words will never pass away. If we live for what we will one day lose, then how can we be fulfilled with those things? However, if we live for what we will never lose, then we can be at peace and filled with joy.

It is one thing to say that Jesus is the foundation for our joy and fulfillment, and it is a completely different thing to live it out each day. We need to know how to live in the joy that Jesus purchased for us on the cross. After telling the Philippians of his desire to know Jesus above all things, Paul went on in chapter 4 to instruct the Philippians in how they should think. What Paul revealed to the Philippians was how to sustain joyful living in Jesus every day. We are to focus our thoughts on that which is true, lovely, and pure. The way we think will eventually dictate both our feelings and actions.

As followers of Jesus, we no longer live like the Old Testament saints. They lived separated from God, illustrated by the veils in the tabernacle and the temple, but when Jesus died, the veil in the temple was torn in two. We now have free access to Father in heaven, just like Jesus does. Paul declared to the Ephesians that we are seated in the heavenly places in Jesus. As there are no barriers between Jesus and Father, so there are no barriers between us and Father. This is more than a theological truth. It dramatically impacts the way that we respond to tribulation and blessing in this world. Rather than fearing difficulties, we recognize them as encounters with Father, because he draws near to the broken-hearted. Rather than fearing the loss of blessings, we use them to bless others and expand the kingdom, just as the first two servants in the parable of the talents. Our life on earth is not meant to be merely survived until Jesus returns or we go to heaven, but it is filled with continual opportunities through difficulties and blessings to develop an ever-increasing intimacy with Father.

While the Jewish nation of the Old Testament lived out the rules written down by Moses, Jesus emphasized living in relationship with our heavenly Father. As we live in relationship with Jesus, Holy Spirit, and Father, we become more transformed to who they are and less conformed to the world. Job declared at the end of his book that he had only heard of God before, but after his encounter with God prompted by the suffering he endured, Job realized that he had seen God and his life was transformed. Before, Job had lived in fear of losing what God had given to him. When he lost everything, he declared that what he had feared happened. Job is much like many religious people today who have much to be thankful for, but live in fear of losing it all. Job learned that knowing God is the most important thing in his life.

Living a transformed life is a continual process. At times, we face the reality that there is still more to go. This is what the disciples discovered when they were unable to heal the demonized boy. Jesus reminded them that, for victory in those situations, they needed prayer. However, Jesus' success in freeing the boy demonstrated it was not prayer as we normally think of prayer. Jesus didn't stop and pray; he commanded the spirit to leave the boy. Prayer for Jesus was not a religious exercise, but communion with Father in heaven. For each new challenge, Jesus depended on new strength from heaven, rather than assuming success, just because he had been successful in the past. Living in a continual dependence upon Father will also protect us from becoming proud of past successes. Samson made this mistake. He enjoyed great success, but he forgot to protect the source of his power. With his hair cut, his relationship with the Spirit of God was hindered, and he was defeated. His past victories did not mean future success. He had to maintain his relationship with heaven. Jesus instructed the disciples to maintain constant contact with heaven through prayer. It is the same type of prayer that we are to practice. As we continually spend time in Father's presence, we will be further transformed to be like Jesus.

Like many of us, Jesus' disciples desired greatness. However, when Jesus asked them about their conversation, they were hesitant to tell him they were arguing about who was the greatest. Rather than telling them not to seek greatness, Jesus told them how to be great. His words are significant. It is OK to seek greatness; we are just to do it in the way that pleases Father. Jesus' definition of greatness is surprising. He told his disciples to be like children. Jesus' words provide contrast to the world's definition of greatness. Children are not considered great by the world. But, to enter the kingdom, the disciples were to trust like children. To be great, the disciples were to be humble like children. This doesn't mean they were to be childish, but childlike. In so doing, Jesus shows a way for his church to overcome much of the division that has plagued those who have followed him through the centuries. His words also free his followers from anxiety that often plagues Christians, as it does those of the world. When Christians choose to live as Jesus teaches, then they will show the world a better way to live. As they do, Jesus will call them great.

Jesus illustrated to us what it means to apply kingdom greatness to our life. Kingdom greatness is not measured in accomplishments and success. Children do not remain sons and daughters by their behavior. They are sons and daughters because of who they are. In the same way, Jesus taught his disciples to rejoice because their names are written in heaven, not because the demons submitted to their commands. Lasting joy always comes through relationship with Father. Kingdom accomplishments are the blessings received from living in communion with Father, just like Jesus lived his life.

Some of Jesus' expressions are difficult to initially understand, like when he told us to strive to enter the kingdom. By this, we know that Jesus did not mean we are to labor and earn our way into the kingdom, but what did he mean? We saw earlier that Jesus' use of striving was similar to pursuing a relationship with him and Father. Paul was an example of this. He was willing to devalue all that was considered important to other people in his life, so that he could know Jesus. If being weak meant knowing Jesus better, then Paul would accept and boast about his weaknesses. Like Paul, we are to seek significance by pursuing a relationship with Jesus in any and all circumstances in our life.

Something else that we often think we understand, but do not completely comprehend, is God's love for us. The most quoted verse in the Bible is John 3:16, "For God so loved the world that he gave his only begotten son that whoever believes in him shall not perish but have eternal life." It is not uncommon for people to be shocked that God would ask Abraham to sacrifice his son, Isaac, because we could never sacrifice our own children. While this reaction is understandable, why are we not shocked that God would sacrifice his son for us? Abraham did what God asked him to do and then stopped him. We should also be shocked at God's actions, but we are not. It is another indicator that we do not fully grasp what God has done for us. When Abraham was willing to sacrifice Isaac, it communicated that Abraham loved God more than he loved Isaac. In the same way, when God sacrificed Jesus, it meant that God loves the world even more than he loves Jesus. That is an extraordinary and life changing truth to comprehend. Every time we are shocked at Abraham's test, we should also be reminded at God's great love for us.

From Abraham's willingness to sacrifice Isaac and God's actual sacrifice of his own son, we learn that God loves us immensely. The next logical question to examine is why he loves us so much. While God's love for us includes the facts that we are in need of his love and we are image-bearers of God, it is more than that. When we examine God's glory, revealed through Scripture, we discover that God's glory is someone. Jesus said that he didn't seek his own glory. That is because he was heavenly glory personified. To seek his own glory would be to seek something lesser than who he already was. Jesus' glory has been given to us who follow him; therefore, we are not to seek our own glory, but recognize who we are. As we discover and live out the implications of being a personification of heavenly glory, it will change the way we live and give purpose to our life.

In Scripture, prophetic words have a powerful impact

upon people's lives. Out of mercy, Father gives us prophetic words to bring about repentance, as he did through Jonah and the Ninevites. On the other hand, he may give us a prophetic word to encourage us to remain faithful in the midst of discouraging circumstances. As we face difficulties in life, it is important to remind ourselves of what God has said to us in the past, so that we will not give up. Jonathan came to David and reminded him that he would be king. Within a short period of time, David faced a crisis in his life. His city was destroyed, and his family was taken into captivity. His men were about to rebel and kill him. But David strengthened himself in the Lord. I believe David reminded himself of what God had said about him. He called his men together. They regained their loved ones and possessions. Within a few weeks, David was king over the tribe of Judah and was clearly on the path that God had declared for him. Without Jonathan's reminder of what God had said about him, David may not have had the strength to keep going, but he did and eventually became king.

In order to live freely in this world, we must also understand "fear." While Scripture tells us to fear God, for it is the beginning of wisdom, it also tells us that perfect love drives out fear. Many Christians have been confused about this seeming contradiction regarding the word "fear." The response is that, like many words, the word "fear" can take on different meanings due to the context. There is something that is a healthy fear, similar to what Jesus told his disciples in Matthew 10:28 when he instructed them not to fear people, but to fear God. That type of fear leads to an increase of love and honor for God our Father. On the other hand, there is an unhealthy fear that leads to condemnation. This is seen in the parable of the talents, when the third servant feared his master because he believed a lie about him. This type of fear leads to anxiety, hiding, and mistrust. This is the type of fear that can be driven away, just as John declared that perfect love drives out fear. As we live in Father's perfect love for us, inappropriate fear will be removed from our life and we will live in joy and freedom.

In Ecclesiastes, Solomon helped us see how many good things in life do not give us satisfaction. Something else is needed! That something is actually someone, Jesus. Jesus' teaching leads us to a transformed life—and that redefines how we are to live. The manner that Jesus lived reveals to us how we are to live out his instruction to be like children without being childish. That way of life defeats despair and opens us up to the possibility of living filled with peace and joy. Rather than living in terror of God, we delight in the presence of our Father. The early Christians transformed Roman society through living sacrificial lives in the service of the sick and abandoned children. Imagine how modern society could be transformed as Christians today fully embrace their position as sons and daughters in the same manner that Jesus did. This is how we've been called to live. Let us go out and do so from this day forward.

Acknowledgments

No project is completed without the support of others. This book is the fruit of many individuals who have contributed in some way. First of all, thank you to my wife, Donelle. Much of this book has been talked through with Donelle over our morning coffee and during conversations on walks and in the car. While I was the one who wrote it down, much of the content is a combination of both our insights. This book was put on hold for several years as I considered how to publish it and who would edit it. Through my daughter, Sara, both questions were answered. A publisher contacted her about book editing, and she recommended them to publish my book. Her suggestions opened up a relationship with Klug Publishing. I also realized that Sara could edit this book as she did with my first book. Although she was in the midst of several other projects, Sara, thankfully, found the time to edit this one for me. At the same time, friends from our church encouraged me to move forward in writing.

Finally, my friend Galen Gingerich, pastor at New Horizons Church in McMinnville, Oregon, has been a constant source of encouragement to keep writing. Thank you all!

About the Author

David Freitag and his wife Donelle currently reside in the San Diego area after having lived in a number of other places. They spent thirteen years in Italy studying and teaching, and after returning to the States in 2000, David was involved in pastoral ministry until 2015. David and Donelle have been married since 1981 and have four grown children.

www.ingramcontent.com/pod-product-compliance
Lightning Source LLC
LaVergne TN
LVHW051517070426
835507LV00023B/3165